How Prayer Can Walk You Through The Storms In Your Life

DR. ESSIE FARLEY

ISBN 978-1-63630-073-3 (Paperback)
ISBN 978-1-63630-074-0 (Hardcover)
ISBN 978-1-63630-075-7 (Digital)

Copyright © 2021 Dr. Essie Farley
All rights reserved
First Edition

All rights reserved. No part of this publication may be reproduced, distributed, or transmitted in any form or by any means, including photocopying, recording, or other electronic or mechanical methods without the prior written permission of the publisher. For permission requests, solicit the publisher via the address below.

Covenant Books, Inc.
11661 Hwy 707
Murrells Inlet, SC 29576
www.covenantbooks.com

Derik and Brittany 8/3/21

May God bless each of you as you go step by step in your journey with God and the storms that you will face in the life ahead of you. God will walk with you as you use this book to assist you.

Essie Finley

To Texas Graduate School of Theology
To Mary P. Greene
I want to thank you for encouraging me in my Christian walk. What a great cheerleader you have been and I thank God for you praying and cheering me along the way. You are truly an example of Christ. My life is blessed because of you. You are an amazing, thoughtful, and kindhearted woman of God. I love you Mary P. Greene.
To Brenda Teehan for reading my book and encouraging me to publish it.
Brenda Teehan, you will always be in my prayers. I love you.

How Prayer Can Walk You through the Storms in Your Life
A dissertation paper submitted in partial fulfillment of
the requirements for the doctoral degree program.

My research is from books and online articles that have encouraged me in my walk with God as well as my past experiences with walking through the storms.

Contents

Foreword 11
Preface 13
1 Introduction 15
    How Prayer Can Walk You through the Storms
    in Your Life 15
2 What Is Prayer? 17
    ACTS: Four Kinds of Prayer 27
    The Benefits of Prayer 32
3 Bring Your Struggling to the Cross 34
4 What Are Storms of Life? 39
    Weathering the Storms of Life 41
5 Counter Argument: What to Do When You Feel God
   Is Not Answering Your Prayer 45
6 God Walks with You Through the Valleys 68
    The Significance of Trials 73
7 Wisdom in the Midst of Trials 90
8 The Holy Spirit 94
    The Nine Fruits of the Holy Spirit 99
9 What Is Faith? 102
    Keeping Faith in Hard Times 108
    Learning to Live by Faith 109
    Choosing Faith Over Fear 110

10	How to Prepare for the Storms of Life	112
11	Seeking Ways to Trust God Through the Storm	115
12	Staying Motivated to Pray in the Storm	117
	The Benefits of Journaling	121
	Having a Positive Mindset for Christ	122
	Renovating Your Mind	123
	Questions You Can Ask God When You Are in a Storm	125
13	The Master's Peace	127
14	The Right Plan from God	139
	Beautiful Diamond	140
15	God Really Does Have a Purpose Behind Your Problems!	143
16	What to Do When the Storm Is Over?	157
	Turning Your Lemon into Lemonade	157
	It Is Time to Turn the Pain into Ministry	158
17	Why Am I Glad God Chastises Me?	161
18	Keep the Dream Alive	163
19	Conclusion	166
References		169

Foreword

My name is Dr. Kenneth R. Greene, senior pastor for M.E.T.R.O. Christ's Church located at 450 E Parkerville Rd. Cedar Hill TX, 75104. It is an honor to write this letter explaining why I selected Ms. Essie Farley to be our prayer warrior minister in the 1990s.

The Apostle Paul's exhortation in Romans 12:12, "Be joyful in hope, patient in affliction, and faithful in prayer," explains the "why" choice of Ms. Farley.

Prayer for M.E.T.R.O. is a foundational expression of faith. We speak but cannot see the one to whom we speak. We listen, not with our physical sense of hearing but, rather, the spiritual inner heart. Jesus says in John 4, "God is Spirit, and those who worship Him must worship in spirit and in truth." The effects of our prayers are often not immediate and, at times, seem ambiguous, at least, from our perspective. Bluntly, we may wonder if prayer does any good.

In Colossians 4:2, Paul offers a similar verse: "Devote yourselves to prayer." In fact, in the Greek, it is the very same phrase. The sense of "devote" implies a strong attachment, allegiance, and affection for someone or something, in this case, prayer and the act of praying. It would include one's passion, time, and needed resources. Ms. Farley is one who is devoted, passionate in her commitment and consistency, and will not be disloyal, inconsistent, or indifferent. This character description should give you a mental picture of Ms. Farley who is devoted to prayer.

"Faithful" is in the present imperative which denotes that we are to follow this command continually, habitually. Being faithful is a continual way of life (lifestyle) for Ms. Farley. Ms. Farley's initial fear to God's call to prayer ministry quickly dissipated when she remembered that whatever God commands of us, He also provides the grace and empowerment through His spirit to carry out. She was reminded that many children of God have abandoned their God-given projects due to challenges encountered while working on those projects. When God gives you a dream, He also gives you a tough life because it takes toughness to achieve greatness. God gives you tough assignments and difficult tasks because it is through tough challenges that God can draw out His potentials within you. She continues to develop her potential by attending prayer workshops in which she returns to develop small groups centered on prayer.

Again, Romans 12:12 tells us to be joyful in hope, patient in affliction, and faithful in prayer during the tough seasons in life. If you are not faithful in prayer, you cannot be joyful in hope; if you are not faithful in prayer, you cannot be patient in affliction. Consequently, the key to withstanding the seasons of adversity is faithfulness in prayer. Which is why I ordained Ms. Farley to give leadership to this ministry. She is a living testimony that God's wisdom, strength, and abilities reside in us. But they do not come out in a place of convenience; they do not come out in a place of comfort; they do not come out when everything is easy. It is through the squeezes of life that our potentials come out; it is through the afflictions of our circumstances that the depth of God's wisdom is released for us. For this reason, Ms. Farley did not faint, nor did she abandon her project.

Understand that Ms. Farley did not abandon her assignment because of the difficulties encountered or the toughness involved. The real reason she did not abandon her assignments, projects, dreams, and faith is because of her devotion to prayer.

Ms. Essie Farley, thanks for being faithful in prayer, and that is why you have successfully ridden the storms of adversity and arrived at your desired destination.

—Dr. Kenneth R. Greene

Preface

As children of God, we would love to go through life without any problems, but life would have no meaning if we did not experience pain and disappointments. God uses the pain and disappointments to shape our lives into what He created us to be. The good news is we have a Savior who is willing to teach us how to manage His benefits so we can walk through the storms of life with peace. Once we learn the benefits God has given to us for the storms, our walk will become less stressful. We will begin to thank Him for the opportunities in the trials He has given to us. We can have a mindset that when the storms come, God is up to something in our lives. We will be able to send up praises to God, knowing blessings will come out of the storms. Our Father will walk through the storms with us because He cares about us.

While living on Earth, we will continue to have pain; it tells us that something is wrong, and we must respond to it. We will not be able to reach our destiny if we do not go through difficulties; we cannot branch out and create ministries that will help someone else. When we walk in pain, it helps us to focus on God and allow Him to change us for His kingdom. We must continue to push—pray until something happens. This is what God wants us to do; He is waiting for us to approach Him with our concerns. Prayer is a weapon that leads to deliverance. Faith is the action that can calm the storm.

Don't you want to know what your purpose is for living here on Earth? Trust God to reveal it to you and use the weapon He has given to you to survive through it. Take the challenge and walk with God as He allows the Holy Spirit to teach you the process.

Introduction

> *How Prayer Can Walk You through the Storms in Your Life*

When I begin my day with God, it seems to set the tone for the rest of the day. It is so amazing how I can have a set time with God before I walk out of my house. I just want to be in His presence and share my pain, thoughts, and needs. I want to wake up saying good morning to my Father and let Him know how excited I am to have Him alongside of me as I walk through the journey. Prayer is about me meditating on God, telling Him how happy I am to be His child. I confess any sin that I am dealing with, and I like to praise Him for who He is. I can have a conversation with God and let Him know I will be available and waiting for His answer. There is no set time that God will answer, but when He does, I always ask that He makes it crystal clear so I will understand on my level. I tell God I do not want to miss any of my blessings, and I want to learn what it is that I need to know about my storm. I ask my Father to help me walk this day as I am trusting and depending on Him.

I keep telling myself what Isaiah 54:17 (KJV) says. "No weapon that is formed against Thee shall prosper; and every tongue that shall rise against Thee in judgment Thou shalt condemn. This is the heritage of the servants of the Lord, and their righteousness is of me, saith the Lord." When I think of no weapon formed against me, and God is in control, it gives me the faith I need to keep praying until God answers my prayer.

During my stormy walks, I listen for His voice as He allows the Holy Spirit to guide me and help me make decisions that are pleasing to Him. I praise God for helping me to get through the morning and request His assistance as I continue throughout the day.

Once I return home and prepare my mind for retiring for the evening, I like to meditate on His Word and thank Him for helping me throughout the day. I can tell God what it is that I had a difficult time with and ask for assistance in handling things better.

Prayer is my energy; it keeps me motivated and connected to God. It is what gives me the peace I need in the storm. I am so glad I am free to speak to God any time I want to. If I am at work and experiencing a difficulty, I can silently pray and ask for His assistance; He is right there with me and waiting for me to request His service. Prayer is what helps remove the stress that occurs in my life from time to time. I can have hope in God that whatever I am dealing with, I can release it to Him, and I begin to feel refreshed. It is like a weight that has been lifted off my shoulder. A weight that is too heavy for me to carry alone.

We are unable to live healthy lives without prayer and be able to walk through storms successfully. God has designed benefits to help us walk through this journey. He is waiting for us to let Him know we need Him. Storms are inevitable, and we have no control over what will come our way. God allows whatever storms He wants, in order to get our attention. We must put our faith in Him and walk with confidence through the storms because He is our physician, and He gives us the medication as we need it.

Prayer is a powerful tool God has given us as our weapon; we must use it to the best of our ability. It takes practice, so we must continue to pray and ask God to help us. This is a battle for you and God, and you must continue to fight, so that means not giving up. God did not design us to be quitters; we are achievers in His eyes. Hang in there, and remember, God will walk with you, and He works all night long. Keep praying so you will grow to have a total dependence on God.

What Is Prayer?

So what is prayer? According to *Webster's Dictionary 1828*, prayer is defined as "in worship, a solemn address to the Supreme Being, consisting of adoration, or an expression of our sense of God's glorious perfections for mercy and forgiveness, intercession for blessings on others, and thanksgiving, or an expression of gratitude to God for His mercies and benefits. A prayer, however, may consist of a single petition, and it may be extemporaneous, written, or printed." Prayer is simply a conversation with God. It is a two-way relationship in which we should not only talk to Him but listen for His will and His promises to be revealed to us.

The Bible tells us in Jeremiah 33:3, "Call unto Me, and I will answer thee, and show thee great and mighty things, which thou knowest not." We must look at prayer as our weapon for spiritual warfare. In 1 Thessalonians 5:17 (KJV), the Bible tells us to "pray without ceasing." In 1 Peter 5:7, the Bible states, "Casting all your care upon Him; for He careth for you." God commands us to pray. If we are going to be obedient to His will, prayer must be a part of our life. There is a lot of power in prayer. You are opening up and telling God what He already knows. He has been waiting to hear from you. When you have a desire to meet with God and share what is going on with you, this is where the passion comes in. You cannot wait to talk with God at the next appointed time. This is when you are devoted to prayer and thankful that God has given you the opportunity to be in His presence. This shows that you have developed a lifestyle of meeting the King, on a daily basis.

Prayer is about coming to God as you are, spilling your guts to Him in a respectful way. If you are unsure of what to say, the Holy Spirit will guide you. Sometimes, we can only mourn and groan; I believe God is pleased if we do. He just wants us to put forth an effort.

In the article by Mary Fairchild, she shares with us how to learn the basic principles of prayer, she writes:

> What Does the Bible Say About Prayer?
>
> Prayer is not a mysterious practice reserved only for clergy and the religiously devout. Prayer is simply communicating with God—listening and talking with Him. Believers can pray from the heart, freely, spontaneously, and in their own words. If prayer is a difficult area for you, learn these basics principles of prayer and how to apply them in your life.
>
> The Bible has a lot to say about prayer. The first mention of prayer is in Genesis 4:26: "And as for Seth, to him also a son was born; and he named him Enosh. The men began to call on the name of the Lord" (NKJV).
>
> What Is the Correct Posture for Prayer?
>
> There is no correct or certain posture for prayer. In the Bible, people prayed on their knees (1 Kings 8:54), bowing (Exodus 4:31), on their faces before God (2 Chronicles 20:18; Matthew 26:39), and standing (1 Kings 8:22). You may pray with your eyes opened or closed, quietly or

out loud—however you are most comfortable and least distracted.

Should I Use Eloquent Words?

Your prayers need not be wordy or impressive in speech: "When you pray, don't babble on and on as people of other religions do. They think their prayers are answered only by repeating their words again and again" (Matthew 6:7 NLT).

"Do not be quick with your mouth, do not be hasty in your heart to utter anything before God. God is in heaven and you are on Earth, so let your words be few" (Ecclesiastes 5:2 NIV).

Why Should I Pray?

Prayer develops our relationship with God. If we never speak to our spouse or never listen to anything our spouse might say to us, our marriage relationship will quickly deteriorate. It is the same way with God. Prayer—communicating with God—helps us grow closer and more intimately connected to God.

"I will bring that group through the fire and make them pure, just as gold and silver are refined and purified by fire. They will call on My name, and I will answer them. I will say, 'These are My people,' and they will say, 'The Lord is our God'" (Zechariah 13:9 NLT).

"But if you stay joined to Me and My words remain in you, you may ask any request you like, and it will be granted" (John 15:7 NLT)!

The Lord instructed us to pray. One of the simplest reasons to spend time in prayer is because the Lord taught us to pray. Obedience to God is a natural by-product of discipleship.

"Keep alert and pray. Otherwise temptation will overpower you. For though the spirit is willing enough, the body is weak" (Matthew 26:41 NLT)!

"Then Jesus told His disciples a parable to show them that they should always pray and not give up" (Luke 18:1 NIV).

"And pray in the spirit on all occasions with all kinds of prayers and requests. With this in mind, be alert and always keep on praying for all the saints" (Ephesians 6:18 NIV).

What If I Don't Know How to Pray?

The Holy Spirit will help you in prayer when you don't know how to pray: "In the same way, the Spirit helps us in our weakness. We don't know what we ought to pray for, but the Spirit himself intercedes for us with groans that words cannot express. And he who searches our heart knows the mind of the Spirit, because the Spirit intercedes for the saints in accordance with God's will" (Romans 8:26–27 NIV).

Are There Requirements for Successful Prayer?

The Bible establishes a few requirements for successful prayer:
- *A humble heart*

"If My people, who are called by My name, will humble themselves and pray and seek My face and turn from their wicked ways, then will I hear from heaven and will forgive their sin and will heal their land" (2 Chronicles 7:14 NIV).

- *Wholeheartedness*

"You will seek Me and find Me when you seek Me with all your heart" (Jeremiah 29:13 NIV).

- *Faith*

"Therefore, I tell you, whatever you ask in prayer, believe that you have received it, and it will be yours" (Mark 11:24 NIV).

- *Righteousness*

"Therefore, confess your sins to each other and pray for each other so that you may be healed. The prayer of a righteous man is powerful and effective" (James 5:16 NIV).

- *Obedience*

"And we will receive whatever we request because we obey Him and do the things that please Him" (1 John 3:22 NLT). (https://www.thoughtco.com.)

In this article by Robert Velarde, he shares with us some reasons to pray, he writes:

1. God's Word Calls Us to Pray

   One key reason to pray is because God commanded us to pray. If we are to be obedient to His will, then prayer must be part of our life in Him. Where does the Bible call us to prayer? Several passages are relevant:
   - "Pray for those who persecute you" (Matthew 5:44 NIV).[1]
   - "And when you pray..." (Matthew 6:5).

---

[1] Unless otherwise noted, all scriptures are from the New International Version of the Bible.

- "This, then, is how you should pray" (Matthew 6:9).
- "Be joyful in hope, patient in affliction, faithful in prayer" (Romans 12:12).
- "And pray in the Spirit on all occasions with all kinds of prayers and requests" (Ephesians 6:18).
- "Do not be anxious about anything, but in everything, by prayer and petition with thanksgiving, present your request to God" (Philippians 4:6).
- "Devote yourselves to prayer, being watchful and thankful" (Colossians 4:2).
- "Pray continually" (1 Thessalonians 5:17).
- "I urge then first of all, that all requests, prayers, intercession and thanksgiving be made for everyone..." (1 Timothy 2:1).

2. Jesus Prayed Regularly

Why did Jesus pray? One reason He prayed was an example so that we could learn from Him. The gospels are full of references to the prayers of Christ, including these examples:
- "After He had dismissed them, He went up on a mountainside by Himself to pray" (Matthew 14:23).
- "Then Jesus went with His disciples to a place called Gethsemane, and he said to them, 'Sit here while I go over there and pray'" (Matthew 26:36).
- "Very early in the morning, while it was still dark, Jesus got up, left the house,

and went off to a solitary place, where He prayed" (Mark 1:35).
- "But Jesus often withdrew to lonely places and prayed" (Luke 5:16).
- "One of those days Jesus went out to a mountainside to pray, and spent the night praying to God" (Luke 6:12).
- "Then Jesus told His disciples a parable to show them that they should always pray and not give up" (Luke 18:1).

3. Prayer Is How We Communicate with God

Prayer allows us to worship and praise the Lord. It also allows us to offer confession of our sins, which should lead to our genuine repentance. Moreover, prayer grants us the opportunity to present our requests to God. All of these aspects of prayer involve communication with our Creator. He is personal, cares for us, and wants to commune with us through prayer.
- "If My people, who are called by My name, will humble themselves and pray and seek My face and turn from their wicked ways, then will I hear from heaven and will forgive their sin and will heal the land" (2 Chronicles 7:14).
- Isaiah wrote, "He gives strength to the weary and increases the power of the weak. Even youths grow tired and weary, and young men stumble and fall; but those who hope in the Lord will renew their strength. They will soar on wings like eagles; they will run and not grow weary; they will walk and not be faint" (Isaiah 40:29–31).

- Hebrews 4:15–16 reads, "For we do not have a high priest who is unable to sympathize with our weaknesses, but we have one who has been tempted in every way, just as we are yet without sin. Let us then approach the throne of grace with confidence, so that we may receive mercy and find grace to help us in our time of need."

Prayer is not just about asking for God's blessings—though we are welcome to do so—but it is about communication with the living God. Without communication, relationships fall apart. So, too, our relationship with God suffers when we do not communicate with Him.

4. Prayer Allows Us to Participate in God's Works

Does God need our help? No. He is all powerful and in control of everything in His creation. Why do we need to pray? Because prayer is the means God has ordained for some things to happen. Prayer, for instance, helps others know the love of Jesus. Prayer can clear human obstacles out of the way in order for God to work. It is not that God can't work without prayers, but that He has established prayer as part of His plan for accomplishing His will in this world.

5. Prayer Gives Us Power Over Evil

Can physical strength help us overcome obstacles and challenges in the spiritual realm? No, "for our strength is not against flesh and blood, but against the rulers, against the authorities, against the powers of this dark world and against the spiritual forces of evil in the heavenly realms" (Ephesians 6:12). But in prayer, even the physically weak can become strong in the spiritual realm. As such, we can call upon God to grant us power over evil.

- "For physical training is of some value, but godliness has value for all things, holding promise for both the present life and the life to come" (1 Timothy 4:8).
- "Watch and pray so that you will not fall into temptation. The spirit is willing, but the body is weak" (Matthew 26:41).

6. Prayer Is Always Available

Nothing can keep us from approaching God in prayer except our own choices (Psalm 139:7; Romans 8:38–39).

7. Prayer Keeps Us Humble Before God

Humility is a virtue God desires in us (Proverbs 11:2, 22:4; Micah 6:8; Ephesians 4:2; James 4:10). Prayer reminds us that we are not in control, but God is, thus keeping us from pride.

- "Therefore, whoever humbles himself like this child is the greatest in the kingdom of heaven" (Matthew 18:4).

8. Prayer Grants us the Privilege of Experiencing God

    Through prayer we obtain an experiential basis for our faith. We do not ignore the intellect or reasons for faith, but prayer makes our experience of God real on an emotional level.

9. Answered Prayer is a Potential Witness

    If our prayer is answered, it can serve as a potential witness for those who doubt.

10. Prayer Strengthens the Bonds Between Believers

    Prayer not only strenghens our relationship with God, but when we pray with other believers, prayer also strengthens the bonds between fellow Christians.

11. Prayer Can Succeed Where Other Means Have Failed

    Have all your options been exhausted? Prayer can succeed where other means have failed. Prayer should not be a last resort but our first response. But there are times when sincere prayer must be offered in order to accomplish something.

12. Prayer Fulfills Emotional Needs

    Do we need God through prayer? Yes! We were made to function best, emotionally, in a prayer relationship with God. As C.S. Lewis puts it, "God designed the human machine to run on Himself. He Himself is the fuel our spirits were designed to burn or the food our spirits were designed to feed on. There is no other."[2]

Prayer then has its reasons, and there are many (https://www.focusonthefamily.com).

ACTS: Four Kinds of Prayer

Here is a list of the four kinds of prayer—ACTS—which stands for adoration, confession, thanksgiving, and supplication.

1. *Prayers of adoration.* I praise God for who He is and tell Him how much I love Him. This is where I tell God to use me for His kingdom.
2. *Prayers of confession.* I pour out my heart to God, I confess any sin that I am aware of, and I ask God to reveal to me any unknown sin in my life so I can ask for forgiveness. I want to make sure my life is free of any sin, and I am living to please God. The Bible tells us in 1 John 1:9 (KJV) that "if we confess our sins, He is faithful and just to forgive us our sins, and to cleanse us from all unrighteousness."
3. *Prayers of thanksgiving.* This is when I begin to thank God for what He is doing in my life—for all the blessings He continues to give me and my family. I also tell Him I look forward to the future blessings because I know He will continue to take care of me.
4. *Prayers of supplication.* Prayer of supplication is a prayer that lifts up requests before God. It is often divided between those requests we make for ourselves (petitions) and those requests we make on behalf of other people (intercessions).

When you look at ACTS, four kinds of prayer, this is a great example for someone who desires to pray and is unsure how to start. It is not about how long your prayer is; remember, God knows all

---

[2] C.S. Lewis. *Mere Christianity* (Macmillan, 1952), book II, chapter 3, "The Shocking Alternative."

about you. This is an opportunity to ask God to teach you how to pray. When you start, He will give you the words. You can also find different prayers in the Bible to pray.

Andrew C. Thompson describes the four kinds of prayer and gives an example of each. He tells us the following:

> Prayer shows up all throughout the Bible. If prayer is a heartfelt conversation with God, then we find it as early as Adam's interactions with God in the Garden of Eden. We also see it as late as the prayer of Jesus Christ to return in glory at the end of the book of Revelation. There are countless examples of individuals offering up prayers to God within the Bible. And this is a whole book of the Bible—the Psalms—that is made up entirely of prayers.
>
> One of the consistent themes in the New Testament's teaching about prayer is that we can be assured that God will hear and respond to our prayers. The apostle John points to this when he says, "This is the confidence we have in approaching God: that if we ask anything according to His will, He hears us" (1 John 5:14 NIV). This is a wonderful message! It tells us that God knows our needs and that God absolutely expects us to bring our needs to Him through prayer.
>
> One way to think about prayer in the Bible is to look at the different types of prayers that we find. Perhaps, the easiest way to think about the major biblical modes of prayer is through the acronym "ACTS." It stands for adoration, confession, thanksgiving, and supplication. The four types of prayer that go by these names are found in many places in the Bible.

HOW PRAYER CAN WALK YOU THROUGH THE STORMS IN YOUR LIFE

Prayers of Adoration

A prayer of adoration is a prayer that praises God's goodness and majesty. In the Bible, we find prayers of adoration in the Psalms, which are often called psalms of praise. For instance, Psalm 111:

"Praise the Lord!

I will give thanks to the Lord with my whole heart, in the company of the upright, in the congregation.

Great are the works of the Lord, studied by all who delight in them.

Full of honor and majesty is his work, and his righteousness endures forever.

He has gained renown by his wonderful deeds.

The Lord is gracious and merciful" (vv. 1–4 NRSV).

Prayers of Confession

A prayer of confession is a searching prayer of the heart. When we confess, we bare our souls before God about our sins and shortcomings. Confession to God is also a model for the kind of mutual confession that believers in the body of Christ are called upon to make to one another (see James 5:16). But ultimately, since all sin is sin against God, we are called to confess our sins to God. A key part of the good news of Jesus is that repentance can bring forgiveness and new life. Indeed, the Bible assures us that sincere confession before God will be met with forgiveness. We see this in 1 John 1:9 which says, "If we confess our sins, He who is faithful and just will forgive us our sins and cleanse us from all unrighteousness" (NRSV). So, prayers of confession ought to be a regular part of our spiritual lives, as we become transformed into the people God would have us be.

Prayers of Thanksgiving

A prayer of thanksgiving is a prayer that recognizes the good things God gives us and offers thanks for them: our health, families, and faith. The apostle Paul told us, "Rejoice always, pray without ceasing, give thanks in all circumstances; for this is the will of God in Christ Jesus for you" (1 Thessalonians 5:16–18 NRSV). A part of what it means to live faithfully is to live out of a deep sense of gratitude for all that God has done for us. Prayers of thanksgiving help us to do that. They give proper thanks to God and shape us into thankful people at our core.

Prayers of Supplication

A prayer of supplication is a prayer that lifts up requests before God. Supplications are often divided between those requests we make for ourselves (petitions) and those requests we make on behalf of other people (intercessions). We can turn again to the apostle Paul, who told us in Philippians, "Do not worry about anything, but with prayer and supplication with thanksgiving let your requests be made known to God" (v. 4:6 NRSV). It is natural for us to ask God for the desires of our hearts, and we can be assured that God will answer our prayers. Just so, we feel the need to pray on behalf of others as well—our family and friends, as well as those whose needs we know even if we do not know them personally. God does answer prayer, even if we need to be mindful that God's answers to prayer are not always the answers, we want God to give!

There are other types of prayer in Scripture beyond the four in the ACTS model. Anyone familiar with the Psalms will know that prayers of lament make up a great part of the Psalms. These lament prayers are a particular type of prayer all their own. In addition, there are particular kinds of prayers of invocation in the Bible, calling upon God to be present in special ways. Prayers of healing fit into this category, as when the letter of James refers to the "prayer of faith" that can heal the sick (see James 5:13–15).

Even so, becoming familiar with the ACTS prayers is a great way to become more familiar with biblical models of prayer in general. When we consider prayer as one of the means of grace, our focus turns to the way Jesus shows us how to pray through His teaching and example in the gospels. We should not be surprised to learn that Jesus's ministry is filled with prayer. He prays in the wilderness after His baptism. He heals a man through prayer. He teaches His disciples to pray. He withdraws to lonely places when He gets overwhelmed by the crowds so He can reconnect with the Father through prayer. He prays at Gethsemane so He might have strength to face His coming crucifixion. And He dies with prayer on His lips, "Into Your hands I commend My spirit."

Jesus's life and ministry are clothed in prayer. In that, He offers us a model of how to live as His followers. He invites us to be a people of prayer. We also find, when we go to the gospels, that Jesus wants us to pray as well. The most precious prayer that we can pray is the prayer that Jesus taught to His disciples. It is called the Lord's Prayer or the "Our Father." It looks like this:

Our Father, who art in heaven, hallowed be Thy name,

Thy kingdom come, Thy will be done, on Earth as it is in heaven.

Give us this day our daily bread.

Forgive us our trespasses,

as we forgive those who trespass against us.

And lead us not into temptation,

but deliver us from evil.

For Thine is the kingdom, and the power, and the glory, for ever and ever.

Amen.

We find Jesus teaching this prayer to His disciples in both Matthew 6:7–15 and Luke 11:1–4. If we want to be counted amongst His disciples today, we ought to offer this prayer to God daily (https://www.seedbed.com/acts-4-kinds-of-prayer-for-the-christian/).

The Benefits of Prayer

The benefit of praying brings answers to our prayers. Daily prayer helps you develop a relationship with God. When you take the opportunity to spend time with Him, He listens and answers. God speaks in mysterious ways. I enjoy riding down the street and finding a sign in the church parking lot that talks about something I have been praying about. I will begin to praise God for answering my prayer. I will park the car, get out, and take a picture of the sign, and when I journal, I like to write the date God answered my prayer.

I had asked a friend of mine to pray for me that when God was ready for me to purchase a home, He will let me know and make it crystal clear. One day, as I was driving down the street passing a church, there was a sign talking about a meeting for homebuyers. I said, "Praise the Lord." I turned my car around, pulled into the church parking lot, took a picture, and sent it to the friend who had been praying for me regarding buying a home. We laughed because we knew what our Father can do.

I also like to ask God to show me where to live, what neighborhood, and who will be my realtor. I believe in God arranging all these services for me. He lined everything up for me, so I did not have to be concerned. The point I am trying to make is I prayed, and then, I listened for God's voice. He told me what to do, how to do it, and when to do it, and I obeyed. Of course, He gave me a beautiful home, and I am happy I listened to Him.

I lost contact with a friend in the past; I could not find her phone number. I began praying and asking God to have her call me. Praise God, I got a call from her, and we just laughed and said what an awesome God we have. This just tells you God can do anything He wants to for His children. I take prayer seriously because I know what it has done for me throughout my life. God has given me the ability to ask for what I need, and I take Him at His word.

I enjoy reading, so when God puts it in my heart to read a book, and He reveals to me an answer to a prayer that I have been waiting on Him to answer, I get motivated; I do not want to put the book down. Once you see how God speaks, you will know what to look for throughout your journey. Here is a list of other benefits from prayer:

1. He comforts us in our affliction.
2. Peace of mind.
3. Gives us hope.
4. Provides wisdom from God.
5. Avoid temptation.
6. Prayer changes us.
7. There is power in prayer.
8. Prayer removes worry and anxiety.
9. It reveals our faith level.
10. With prayer, we are able to view problems as opportunities

3

Bring Your Struggling to the Cross

In this article by Jack Hayford, he encourages us to take our struggles to the cross. He writes the following:

> "Abba, Father, all things are possible for You. Take this cup away from me; nevertheless, not what I will but what you will" (Mark 14:36).
>
> There is a relationship between struggling and character. The Cross is the Holy Spirit's primary instrument for shaping our character. The events in Gethsemane represent a Man who, although the sinless Son of God, was aware that what He asked for wasn't why He was there—still cries out for reprieve from the Cross.
>
> Jesus wasn't seeking to escape His responsibility. He was struggling with the horrendous pressure of a situation any human being would rather avoid. It isn't cowardice or rebellion. It was a human being experiencing His life's purpose hammered out on an anvil of circumstance, and

it was going to cost Him His life. He was asking if it could be worked out another way.

We've all gone through tough times in which we've said to God, "I don't want this to happen to me." Under those pressures, many abandon their availability to process, but Jesus didn't.

We each face, at some time in life, a pivotal moment that arises from the commitment we've made to the Lord's way, even though everything in us screams for our own way. It involves a kind of dying, a surrender of things. Our serve-your-own-interest society argues against this surrender. Apart from a careful assessment of Jesus and His approach to the Cross, this same self-gratification creeps into the lives of believers and crumbles the foundations of many who end up far removed from what the Lord has created them to be in Him.

God wants to do a redemptive work through you

God is not just building your character, but as He did with His Son, God is seeking to work something redemptive through you. It will cost you to become an instrument of redemption. When it's over, anything you thought you were losing will be fully recovered, plus more than you can imagine.

As Jesus went to the Cross, considering the cost to Himself, He was not asking for a way out on His own terms—the terms are scriptural: Father, all things are possible to You. We often miss the fact that within Jesus was both the eternal God and a human being. His sinlessness is not altered by this encounter, but His humanness is screaming out loud in Gethsemane. Unless we can capture a reality of what was spoken three times by Jesus, we won't understand how entirely acceptable it is to God when your heart cries out in struggles and looks for a way out.

Learning how to bring our struggling to Christ's Cross is to recognize that there's nothing of your struggle that is unwelcome in heaven or unwilling to be heard by the Father.

Identifying with Jesus's struggle is recognizing that He is bringing His agony before the Father. When we have a struggle, many times, we opt to manage in a way other than the will of God. The struggle isn't brought to the Lord. We don't say, "Father if this is possible…" We say, "Father, this is impossible, and so I'll just do it my own way." Such is the way of the flesh to try and find justification before God for us to do it our own way rather than saying, "Lord, I'll come the way of the Cross."

Intimacy and willingness

The intimacy relationship is found in Jesus's opening words of this prayer: "Abba, Father." They describe His trust in and availability to the Father, and His readiness to reach up and take "Daddy's" hand for support.

If there were another way, would not our Heavenly Father have delighted in sending 10,000 angels to rescue His Son from this moment? But there was no other way. When the only way out is through, are you still able to call God "Daddy?"

Your character provides the answer. You will say "No," unless your character has been shaped by Calvary. "Nevertheless, not what I will, but what You will" are not words of resignation. They are words of intimate trust and willing commitment.

Outbreak and overflow

There are times in our lives when everything argues for another course, but deep in the integrity of your heart, you know that isn't the Father's way. The living Jesus, who has come to forgive us and save us, comes to live in us to give us the same strength of character He had. Having made the choice of the Cross and paid the price of that struggle, two things were unleashed: the outbreak of redemption and the revelation of eternal life and glory.

Because Jesus chose the Father's will, full redemption and salvation broke open on this planet. Three days later came a manifest, explosive breakthrough of life crushing the power of hell and, for all time, opening the gates of glory to the redeemed.

Bring your struggling to the cross

Whenever you and I bring our struggling to the Cross and opt for the Father's way rather than our own, an outbreak of God's redemptive purposes is made possible. You can't imagine the impact your submission to His way will have in the redemption of other people. You are not their Savior, but you're an instrument of His saving grace.

When we bring our struggling to the Cross in obedience, we experience a glorious outbreak of His resurrection, blessing in our own souls, and also experience it flowing through and beyond us (https://www.jackhayford.org/teaching/articles/bring-your-struggling-to-the-cross).

4

What Are Storms of Life?

A spiritual storm is a trial, tragedy, or misfortune. The trials have a purpose in our lives, and when you stay on board, you will learn the reason for the pain. Storms can either make us or break us, depending on how we respond. Storms are a training process for God's children. He uses the storms to shape us into who He wants us to be. He is our physician, giving us our medication as needed. Storms are those things that make us feel uncomfortable and causes us to believe that our pain is unbearable. Pain is how we know something is wrong, and we must act on it and allow God to assist us as He chooses.

Merriam-Webster Online defines trial(s) as a test of faith, patience, or stamina through subjection to suffering or temptation.

We must understand that there are two types of storms; one is the storm that we create for ourselves, and it is called a correcting storm. The second one is perfecting storm which is the storm that comes due to us being in the will of God (http://www.merriam-webster.com).

In the book *Advancing Through Adversity*, Charles Stanley shares with us how God limits the adversity in our lives. He writes:

> Although God may allow Satan to persecute us and harass us, God also puts a limit on the amount of adversity He allows Satan to send our

way. In the case of Job, the Lord stopped Satan the first time with the limitation of "do not lay a hand on his person" (Job 1:12), and the second time with the limitation of "spare his life" (Job 2:60). Satan had to comply with God's command both times, and Satan has to comply today with God's limitations on the amount of adversity you and I experience as God's children. That's good news for us. There is a limit to adversity. It will come to an end.

Today's troubles are just that—today's troubles. A season of trouble is just that—a season of trouble. Crises pass, circumstances change, and situations evolve.

Daniel noted this in his prophetic word when he said that the "beast" would be allowed to persecute the saints "for a time and times and half a time" (Daniel 7:23-25). The word *persecute* in this passage literally means "wear out." The enemy of our souls' attempts to grind us down, wear us out, and wring us dry. But God says, "Not completely." There is nothing Satan can do to us or in us beyond a point if we will continue to trust God and resist the devil.

Furthermore, the Lord does not allow us to be tempted or persecuted beyond our ability to endure it (Stanley, Charles, *How to Handle Adversity*, 1989).

What good news this is! God will provide a way of escape from our trials and tribulations.

When I am in the midst of a storm, it can be very painful at times. I must say I have had some storms that made me feel like my insides were on fire, and I went to God in tears, crying out for help. I just wanted peace to be able to stand the tough times. Of course, I wanted a way out immediately; who wants to feel like they are in a

HOW PRAYER CAN WALK YOU THROUGH THE STORMS IN YOUR LIFE

box that has been set on fire? No one, but God came to my aid and helped me. I expressed how I desired to learn from the storm what He wanted me to know, but I needed help. This was the time when I clung to God in prayer, due to my pain. I needed to sit before Him until He was ready to tell me what to do.

Each day, I would meet with God, meditate on His Word, pray, and listen for Him to speak to me through the Holy Spirit. The Holy Spirit guided me and kept me on track as I walked through the storm. This helped me to stay calm and have the peace I needed as I walked through the storm. I noticed, as before, I continued to sit at the Lord's feet and listen to Him, I stayed in peace. Every time Satan tried to tell me no, God will not provide what I need, I stood on the promises of God and told Satan he is a liar. I told him I know what God can and will do for me.

I read several chapters of Psalms during this stormy time in my life because it brought me peace. These chapters kept me connected to God in a very personal way. When Satan tried to tell me something, I got up and ran for my Bible and began reading the Word, which is my weapon to fight back.

I have a picture hanging in my bathroom, and from time to time, I just stand in front of the picture and meditate on the words which reads, "When you saw only one set of footprints, it was then that I carried you." These words bring joy to my heart. It gives me a reason to be thankful in the storm. This is where I can praise God for who He is and what He does for me. When I think of the Lord's footprints, it reminds me that He is watching over me and providing my every need. I like to take a picture of the footprint words and have it on my cell phone screen, so every time I pick up my phone, it will remind me that I am being cared for.

Weathering the Storms of Life

In this article by Charles F. Stanley, he shares with us four lessons to learn as we are faced with storms in our lives. He states the following:

Reflecting on the divine purpose in hardship can help us respond to trials in a God-honoring way as we seek to understand the lessons He wants us to learn through life's dark moments.

The disciples experienced several "mountaintop moments" in their time with Jesus. But when a storm arose while they were out on the Sea of Galilee, fear took over. Amidst the roaring waves and with the boat rocking, Jesus's chosen ones failed to recall the lessons they had learned about the power and purposes of their leader. Even the appearance of Christ walking on water didn't bring immediate relief (Matthew 14:26).

When trouble strikes, we sometimes forget our knowledge of God, too. We struggle to recall past answers to prayer, specific guidance provided by the Holy Spirit, and lessons learned in previous crises. Only the present seems real. Our minds spin with future implications, and our troubled emotions inhibit clear thinking. In our own strength, we lack sufficient resources and abilities to meet life's challenges. So, God provides what we need. Our suffering is never a surprise to the Lord. He knows everything we are going through. More than that, He is orchestrating our circumstances for His glory and our benefit, according to His good will.

Let us take a moment to fix our attention on the Lord and seek to understand four lessons He wants us to learn through life's dark moments:

1. One purpose for hardships is cleaning. Because of our own "flesh" nature and the self-absorbed world we live in, it's easy to develop selfish attitudes, mixed-up priorities, and ungodly habits. The pressures that

bear down on us from stormy situations are meant to bring these impurities to our attention and direct us to a place of repentance. Our trials are intended to purify and guide us back to godliness, not ruin our lives.

2. A second reason we face difficulty is, so we'll be compassionate and bring comfort to others. God's work in our lives is not intended solely for us. It's designed to reach a world that does not recognize or acknowledge Him. The Lord uses our challenges to equip us for serving others. As we experience suffering, we will learn about God's sufficiency, His comforting presence, and His strength to help us endure. Our testimony during times of difficulty will be authentic. Those to whom we minister will recognize that we know and understand their pain. What credibility would we have with people in crisis if we never experienced a deep pain?

3. Third, God promises us He will provide a path through any trial we face. The disciples probably wondered how long the storm would last and whether they would make it safely to shore. Most likely, they wished it never happened. But had they somehow avoided this storm, they would have missed the demonstration of Jesus's power over the sea and wind. The frightening situation was transformed into a revelation of the Savior's divine nature. God wants to make His power known through our trials as well.

4. The most important thing He gives us is awareness of His presence. At first, the disciples believed they were alone in a terrifying storm. When they initially spotted Jesus, their fear increased. They thought He was a ghost. But as they recognized Him, their fear changed to relief and hope. Similarly, we may not sense God's presence during a crisis, but He has promised to always be with us (Hebrews 13:5–6).

The assurance that the Lord will never leave provides immediate comfort, an infusion of courage and a sense of confidence to endure.

No one enjoys suffering, but in the hands of the Almighty God, trials become tools. He uses hardships to shape believers into the people He intends them to be. Jesus allowed the disciples to experience the fear and anxiety of being in a boat on a raging sea. He permitted them to suffer because He had something far more important to teach them. He wanted the disciples to recognize their own helplessness, His sufficiency, and their dependence on Him.

Ask God to reveal His abiding presence in the midst of your trouble. And remember—He always provides for your spiritual needs to help you both endure and grow stronger in your Christian faith (https://www.intouch.org).

Counter Argument: What to Do When You Feel God Is Not Answering Your Prayer

In the book *God Will Make a Way* by Terry Rush, he tells us God has not abandoned us. He shares the following information: God is right beside you and has been there all along. God cares for us.

God does not minimize your pain

Matthew 6:34 reads, "Therefore do not be anxious for tomorrow; for tomorrow will care for itself. Each day has enough trouble of its own."

The Lord knows this stuff is hard for you. He knows because He sent Jesus to interpret human hurt. He sampled it. The report Jesus filed in heaven was, "It's difficult—at times beyond bearing." God does not advise, "Do not regard as difficult," but rather, "Do not be anxious." The Lord is not in denial. Neither does He expect you to be.

He has been there...ahead of you

In the midst of crisis, your mind floods with questions. Does God care? Where was He when I needed Him? What has He done to help me in my personal trial? Frustration builds. But be encouraged. Not only is God aware, He has been there in the depths of your ruin... ahead of time. He has worked to make a way.

Does God care? God demonstrates His love for you in that He allowed Jesus to know your pain. Jesus's experience on the cross puts Him in the center of your crisis—tasting it, wearing it, measuring it, enduring it, dying with you over it...ahead of time...at Calvary.

Where was God when you needed Him? Centuries earlier, He was carrying out the plans to deal with your specific crisis—plans that would provide avenues for your survival. God was working on your case before your nightmare began.

What did God do for your personal trial? He walked in your shoes before you had feet. He knows your shoe size. He was there to presuffer your pain in order to know exactly how to pay the bill...your bill. Not only has He provided heaven in the long run, He offers hope for the present.

Your divorce, tumor, depression, loss, disappointment, and your greatest fear all had His undivided attention before you experienced them. Before you hit your crisis, He was there like an insurance adjuster estimating the damage, weighing your needs, and preparing your solution. He is also waiting for you at your next tragedy and your next one.

God makes a way when there seems to be no way. He is not the Red Cross that comes to the site of the disaster after it occurs. He comes from the cross; He is not only there before you arrive at the scene, He is there ahead of the scene. Referring to the intense attention of our invisible Father, David Redding said, "Before God ever created Earth, and risked the cry that came from there, He had already determined that He could handle it." The cross would not be too big for Him to carry, nor the stone too large to roll away. He knew all along, as Christ sweat through Gethsemane and struggled up that last hill, that He would rise again; and He declared, 'Let there be light,' this time there would be light the darkness could not overcome. God had the answer long before Adam and Eve bothered about the apple (*God Will Make A Way*. Howard Publishing Co., Inc. 1995, pp. 48–50).

Joyce Meyer shares with us from her book *Enjoying Where You Are on the Way to Where You Are Going*. She shares the following:

Joy in God's Waiting Room

"A man's mind plans his way, but the Lord directs his steps and makes them sure" (Proverbs 16:9).

We think and plan in temporal terms, and God thinks and plans in eternal terms. What this means is that we are extremely interested in right now, and God is much more interested in eternity. We want what "feels good" right now, what produces immediate results, but God is willing to invest time. God is an investor; He will invest a lot of time in us because He has an eternal purpose planned for our lives.

God sees and understands what we don't see and understand. He asks us to trust Him, not to live in carnal reasoning and be frustrated because things don't always go according to plan.

Without abundant trust in God, we will never experience joy and enjoyment. We have ideas about how and when things should happen. Not only does God have a predetermined plan for our lives, but He has the perfect timing for each phase. Psalm 31:15 assures us that our times are in His hands. Fighting and resisting the timing of God is equivalent to fighting His will.

Many times, we fail to realize that being out of God's timing is the same as being out of His will. We may know what God wants us to do, but not when He wants us to do it.

Abraham had a very definite word from God about his future. He knew what God had promised but had no word regarding when it would take place.

The same is often true for us. While we are waiting for our manifestation to come forth—waiting for the breakthrough—it is not always easy to enjoy the time spent in the waiting room.

Once God speaks to us or shows us something, we are filled up with it. It is as though we are "pregnant" with what God has said. He has planted a seed in us, and we must enter a time of preparation. This time prepares us to handle the thing that God has promised to give us or do for us.

It is very much like the birth of a child. First, the seed is planted in the womb, then come nine months of waiting, and finally, a baby is born.

HOW PRAYER CAN WALK YOU THROUGH THE STORMS IN YOUR LIFE

During those nine months, there is a great deal that is happening. The woman's body is changing to prepare her to be able to give birth. The seed is growing into maturity. The parents are preparing things in the natural for the baby's arrival. They are accumulating the necessary equipment to properly care for a child.

Just as there is a lot of activity inside the mother's body that we cannot see, so there is a lot of activity in the spiritual world concerning God's promises to us. Just because we cannot see or feel anything happening does not mean that nothing is taking place. God does some of His best work in secret, and He delights in surprising His children.

The Lord Will Come Suddenly!

"Behold, I send My messenger, and he shall prepare the way before Me. And the Lord [the Messiah], whom you seek will suddenly come to His temple; the messenger or angel of the covenant Whom you desire, behold, He shall come, says the Lord of hosts" (Malachi 3:1).

You may be seeking God and waiting on God. Don't give up! God comes suddenly! Your "suddenly" may be today or tomorrow.

God loves you, and He definitely has a good plan for your life. Believe it! Expect it!

"Put your hope in Him, and you will never be disappointed or put to shame. (Romans 5.5).

The Silent Years

There is an appointed time. Only God knows exactly when it is, so settle down and enjoy the trip. Enjoy where you are on the way to where you are going!

We all have times when we feel that nothing is happening, and it seems that no one, not even God, really cares. We can't seem to hear from God. We can't "feel" God.

We wonder if we are a little "flaky," or maybe we never heard from God after all.

Those are times when it seems as if God has placed us neatly on a shelf, and we wonder if He will ever use us, or if we will ever experience our breakthrough.

Waiting! Waiting! Waiting!

It sometimes seems to us that we have waited forever. We grow weary and don't feel that we can hang on much longer, and then, something happens—maybe just a little something.

Like the Prophet Elijah, we see a cloud the size of a man's hand on the horizon (1 Kings 18:44), and it gives us confidence that it really is going to rain.

Perhaps your "cloud" is a special word from God that someone gives you, or perhaps you are touched by God in a specific way. Perhaps a gift comes—something for which you have been believing—that only God knew about, and it encourages you that you are alive and waiting.

Maybe you are called to preach and receive an invitation to speak at the men's fellowship or the women's prayer group at church. The invitation renews your hope that doors are beginning to open.

The "silent years" were difficult, but very necessary. I was growing, gaining wisdom, experience, learning how to come under authority, and learning the Word that I was called to preach.

Just when I was about ready to give up, the wind of God would blow by. He would do something to keep me hoping.

God is closely watching over the lives of His children, and He will never allow more to come on us than we can bear. (1 Corinthians 10:13.) God provides the way out of every situation in due time. In the meantime, He will give us what we need to be stable and joyful if we will trust Him for it, realizing that He knows best (*Enjoying Where You Are on the Way to Where You Are Going.* Warner Books. 2002, pp. 157–174).

In this book, *The Power of Praying Together*, by Stormie Omartian with Jack Hayford. It begins with the following:

What Should I Do If My Prayers Are Not Answered?

There are many different reasons why our prayers are not answered. It may be that they just haven't been answered yet because the timing isn't right for the answer to come.

Or perhaps we have prayed something that is not God's will. Or our prayers have been answered, but we can't see it because they weren't answered the way we thought they would be.

Sometimes, our prayers are not answered because we ask from a wrong heart.

Perhaps our heart harbors unforgiveness toward someone. "If I regard iniquity in my heart, the Lord will not hear" (Psalm 66:18). Perhaps our heart is selfish, or our motivation is off. "You ask and do not receive, because you ask amiss, that you may spend it on your pleasures" (James 4:3).

Jesus promised that if we will spend time with Him, learn from Him, get to know Him, be honest with Him, and acknowledge our sin against Him, then we can ask of Him whatever we want and He will answer. "If you abide in Me, and My words abide in you, you will ask what you desire, and it shall be done for you" (John 15:7). The key is wanting what He wants. When we do that, we end up doing His will and we find our prayers answered.

When I first came to know the Lord, I prayed about everything and was disappointed when all my prayers weren't answered. As I matured in the things of God, I realized that He and I are on the same side, and my praying is actually working in partnership with Him to see His will done on Earth. Then I became more consistent in prayer and not so disappointed if my prayers weren't answered immediately or exactly the way I prayed them. I trusted Him to answer in the time and way He chose. I concentrated on the praying instead of on the answers. It was freeing.

Once you have prayed, release your concerns. This doesn't mean you can't pray about the same thing again, but once you've finished a prayer, allow the issue to be surrendered into His hands so you can rest and be at peace. Don't worry about whether He heard you or if you did it right. Trust Him to take care of it. Learn to partner with God.

"For the eyes of the Lord run to and fro throughout the whole Earth, to show Himself strong on behalf of those whose heart is loyal to Him" (2 Chronicles 16:9). You'll see more power

HOW PRAYER CAN WALK YOU THROUGH THE STORMS IN YOUR LIFE

in your prayers when you partner with others (Omartian, Stormie and Jack Hayford, *The Power of Praying Together*. 2009, 66–67).

When I am in the midst of a trial and I feel like God is not answering, I keep praying and keep trusting. I continue to stand on His word and His promises. Then, I continue to pray until something happens, which means never give up. God will answer; it may not be when we want Him to, but it will always be right on time. Our prayers have to line up with His will for our lives, so persevere until the end. You just keep praising Him for taking care of you and remind yourself of a previous storm in your life when God answered.

Look for ways to be surprised by your prayers. I cry out to God and command my blessing, not in a rude way, but I want God to know I need Him to help me, and I am going to stand on His promises and trust Him until something happens. I tell God I am available and ready to listen and hear from Him about my situation. I like to get my Bible and all my study tools, along with a good cup of coffee, and sit before God. I pour out my heart to Him and wait for Him to reveal whatever He wants to. There is power in the word *prayer*, and we must use the resources available to us. When He reveals what He wants to me, I like to journal about it so I can use it for encouragement or share with others at a later time. When I get ideas of new things to try in my life, I begin working on them and telling God how thankful I am for revealing these things to me. Jesus tells us that His power works best in our weakness. I can't think of a better time to use this power, especially in the midst of storms. When you have done all that you can do, God will do the rest.

I always try to keep in mind that this life is not about me; it is about God and what He wants to do with me. When I feel like He is not answering my prayers, I ask Him why. He will reveal it to me. I tell God to reveal to me any sin I knowingly or unknowingly did in my life so I can repent of it. Sometimes, God reveals the answer to me, and it may not be what I want to hear. I pray and ask Him to help me in this area because I want my life to be in line with His will. I ask Him to remove whatever needs to be removed so it can be replaced with what He wants. He also tells me not right now to some of my prayers. It is not saying no; He is only saying now is not the time. So, I tell Him to let me know when the time is right, and I continue on with my life.

God knows what will occur in my life and when He will bring it all together. I can rest in assurance that when He reveals to me the right time, I can look back and say yes, God knew all along, and He answers right on time. I have to keep in mind that I may not be ready for this answer in a mature way or not know what to do with it, until God works on me in another area of my life.

I am always praying that God reveals things to me step by step. This seems to work in my life if I am praying about something on a long-term basis such as my destiny. I recall telling God I wanted to leave the nursing home setting. I told Him I did not want anything else to do with a nursing home for the rest of my life, and I left. Years later, while spending time with Him, I felt He had something else He wanted to teach me before I left. I had a conversation with Him one day, and it led me to say to Him, "If You want me to return, I will." I also told Him, "If You want me to return, then have someone to call me for a job in the nursing home. A few months later, I received a call from this young lady who I did volunteer work with; she stated she spoke with an administrator who is looking for a social worker. She said she told him about me, and he wants me to call him today. I immediately said, "Look at God." I was in a meeting down the street from this nursing home and had on a pair of jeans, so I did not want to visit the nursing home. I called and spoke with the administrator, and he asked if I could come in for an interview today. I explained to him that I was in a social workers' meeting, and I had on jeans. He said it was okay and to come anyway. At this point, all I could think about was what I told God, and I am seeing how He is arranging an interview for me. This shows how we have no idea of when God will answer our prayers or how.

We must trust that He is working, and when the time is right, He will let us know. I told myself before I went to the interview, *This is what I have been praying about. If God wants me to return, He will allow me to receive a call.* I went to the nursing home and spoke with the administrator, and we agreed on the job, salary, and a start date. This experience gave me more motivation to pray step by step for direction for my life.

As I began the new job, I continued to pray for the next step in my destiny. One day, as I was walking down the hall on my job, God revealed to me to go to school to become a chaplain. I said, "What!" I was excited, so I Googled the word *chaplain* to look at all the duties of this role. I could not wait to see what school was available for me to attend. I knew this was God, and I wanted to be obedient. I continued to pray and called different schools to see where God wanted me to go. I started school the next semester, and now, I am getting my doctoral degree. All the praises go to God. I look forward to seeing what He does with me and through me. This shows how I continued in prayer and allowed the Holy Spirit to guide me step by step through the process.

In the book *How to Listen to God* by Charles Stanley, he shares with us some ways we can hear what God is saying to us. He shares the following:

Are Your Listening?

Patiently

God will not tell us some things instantaneously. We will hear some special revelations only after having waited a season of time. One of the reasons is simply that we're not always ready. Because of that, God will sometimes withhold information until we are prepared to listen.

We must be willing to listen to Him patiently because these times may draw out and stretch our faith. He has promised to speak to our hearts so we can expect Him to, but He is not compelled to tell us everything we want to know the moment we desire the information.

We'd like to say, "Lord, here's my order today. Please give me an answer before I get up off my knees." It may be weeks later before God speaks to us about this, not because He has forgotten, but because in the process of waiting, He is changing and preparing us to hear His message, which we may not have received had He spoken instantaneously.

Actively

To hear God, we must actively wait and meditate upon His Word. Colossians 3:16 declares, "Let the Word of Christ dwell in you richly in all wisdom, teaching, and admonishing one another in psalms and hymns and spiritual songs, singing with grace in your hearts to the Lord." If we only know the Word selectively and dwell on one particular favorite subject, we fail to seek the whole counsel of God. The way we become wealthy and overflowing with the truth of the Word is to meditate upon Scripture, search it out, digest it, and apply it to our hearts.

God is so precise in His instructions and promises given through His Word. Meditation upon God's Word is one of the most wonderful ways we can listen to the voice of God for divine guidance.

Confidently

We must be confident that when we listen to God, we will hear what we need to hear. It may not always be what we wish to hear, but God communicates to us what is essential in our walk with Him.

HOW PRAYER CAN WALK YOU THROUGH THE STORMS IN YOUR LIFE

Dependently

As we come to God, we must come in recognition that we are totally dependent upon the Holy Spirit to teach us truth. If we come to Him with a prideful attitude, it will be difficult for the Holy Spirit to instruct us.

There's no way for us to hear from God apart from the ministry of the Holy Spirit. When God speaks through others or through circumstances, it is the work of the Spirit.

Submissively

We need to listen to God submissively, because sometimes when He speaks to our heart, we will not like what we hear. When the Lord tells us something we don't want to hear, we may not react in total obedience. But God doesn't get hostile over our rebellious spirits, that's not His response. He knew us before we ever came to listen to Him, and He knew exactly how we would respond.

Reverently

A reverent heart should be the foundation of hearing God. We should be in awe that we can speak to the God who hung the sun and world on nothing, the God who created all the intricacies of human life.

We should be humble that this same omnipotent God is quietly willing to listen to us while simultaneously giving direction to the vastness of the universe. His total, concentrated, and undisturbed attention is focused upon us individually.

That ought to humble us and create within us a reverence that acknowledges God for the mighty Creator He is (Stanley, Charles, *How to Listen to God*. 1985, pp. 82–91).

In this article by Gary DeLashmutt, "Asking according to God's will," he shares with us that God is offering us an amazing resource. He tells us the following:

Asking According to God's Will

The key condition is according to God's will. In 1 John 5:14–15, the Bible indicates we can be confident that God will grant our requests when they are according to His will. John is echoing what he heard Jesus promise in John 16:23. To pray in Jesus's name is not a magical incantation that obligates Jesus to grant your wish—it is to ask as a representative of Jesus, who was always answered because he always asked according to God's will.

In this sense, request prayer is one aspect of what theologian's call "human agency." God has a plan to redeem humanity and reestablish His kingdom through Jesus. And He has decided to accomplish this plan (to an amazing degree) through human agents—people who voluntarily cooperate with Him. This is why most people meet Jesus through the agency of other Christians who show them Jesus's love and tell them how Jesus has changed their lives. This is why most mature Christian workers have been developed through the agency of other Christian workers who inspired, motivated, trained, and coached them. But the ground floor of all human agencies is requested prayer—as we ask God to act according to His will, He does so by intervening and mobilizing His agents. This is why all significant spiritual work must be birthed and bathed in prayer!

How do you pray according to God's will? Without removing the complexity and mystery, I want to suggest that it involves three things that are interrelated and dynamically influence one another: entrusting ourselves to God's loving authority, praying in line with God's Word, and being led by God's Spirit.

Entrust yourself to God's loving authority

The most basic way that we ask according to God's will is to adopt the proper heart attitude—we entrust ourselves to God's loving authority. This involves humbly putting yourself under God as your rightful leader, choosing to trust that His will is right and good (even if you don't know what it is), and aligning your heart to follow Him. Jesus calls this praying that "the Father may be glorified" (read John 14:13).

Focus on God's priorities

Besides cultivating the proper attitude in prayer, we also need to pray for the right things. Asking according to God's will involves focusing on God's priorities. The Bible not only informs us of specific things that are or are not God's will—it also reveals what God says is important. The more your perspective is soaked in God's Word, the more you will pray according to its priorities, and the more you will see God answer your requests (John 15:7).

When we don't know God's priorities, we will naturally pray for our own priorities—which centers around getting more pleasant circumstances, having people treat us the way we want to be treated, and getting relief from irritating and painful circumstances or people. If this is what dominates your prayer requests, your batting average is going to be pretty low, and your motivation to pray is going to diminish. Begin to pray primarily for God's priorities—and see what happens! Here are some examples:

- Ask God for more practical insight into Scripture so you can become more godly in character (Psalm 119:33–34).
- Ask God for greater love for other people (1 Thessalonians 3:12) and better discernment on how to love them effectively (Philippians 1:9).
- Ask God for wisdom to understand what He wants to teach you through the adverse circumstances He has allowed in your life (James 1:5).

Ask God's Spirit to help you

Asking according to God's will also involves asking God's Spirit to help you. This is what Paul and Jude call "praying in the Spirit" (Ephesians 6:18 and Jude 1:20). This is the most subjective part of requested prayer, and the most easily abused ("God led me to pray for a new spouse")—but it is a key part, nonetheless. Read Romans 8:26 and 27. Since we don't know how to pray, God's Spirit helps us to pray by interceding for us according to God's will. As we talk to God, entrusting ourselves to His loving author-

> ity, and as we pray according to the priorities in His Word, His Spirit guides us to pray more specifically for the things He wants to do.
>
> This is one reason why praying with other Christians is so important. Read Matthew 18:19 and 20. When we pray together "in My name" (submitted to His will, in line with His priorities), Jesus is present among us through His Spirit to guide us so that we "agree" (lit. "symphonize") on how to pray for specific matters. We can better discern the Spirit's guidance when we pray with one another than when we pray alone. I see this happen regularly at our home group's prayer on Sunday nights. Someone will pray for a person or a situation in a certain way, then someone else will pray about the same thing—but in a different way that is more biblical in perspective. As we pray together about these matters, our prayers become more specific, and there is a growing sense that this is God's will. I mark such prayers in my mind—and note how God answers them (even though often not immediately). (https://www.xenos.org/teachings/?teaching=1032).

If you feel God has not answered your prayer, keep praying and do not take matters in your own hands. You will be disappointed. Ask God to show you what you are unable to see clearly. God can send another person to speak to you about things that need your attention. There are times in our lives where God wants us to be still. He is telling us just wait for Him. He knows the outcome; when He is ready to move you to the next level, He will. We live in a world where we can get things in a few minutes. God has a process that He wants to take us through so we can stay on His path. When we stay on His path, it brings joy to His heart.

When you attempt to take matters in your own hands, you are telling God you do not trust Him. You are setting yourself up for more pain. God wants to help you, not cause you unnecessary pain or disappointment. Here is an example of a time in my life when I tried to take things into my own hands.

I had been praying for a job and wondered if God wanted me to return to Dallas. Well, I did not wait for Him to tell me yes, no, or maybe. I just kept praying and applying for jobs in Dallas. When I applied for the jobs in Dallas, they had the same type of job openings in San Antonio and Austin, Texas. Each time I would apply for a job, I got a call for an interview, and I went to the interview but returned home somewhat disappointed. When I think of the money, I spent to go on these interviews out of town, hotel stays, and food, I could have used that money for something else.

This is what happens when we step out of line and don't wait upon God. This is the reason why, when I pray now, I ask God to make it crystal clear so I will understand on my level. While I am continuing to wait on God, I find a good book to read about waiting on the Master's answer and get my scripture and place it in my shoe. At this point, I had stopped looking for a job altogether and just prayed. I repented of my sin and rested my head on my Father's shoulder. I wanted Him to know how sorry I was for what I did. This is another reason why I like step-by-step directions. I do not always get it correct when I am listening to God. The key point is I repented and corrected my mistake.

I was invited to Dallas to a church function one week, so I went, and I enjoyed myself. One of the ladies came over to the table and told me if I ever want to move back to Dallas, just let her know. I told her, "No, I am happy where I am." I told God I do not want to move back to Dallas. I will wait for Him to show me what He has in mind.

I was excited; I got back on track because God gave me a new job, right here in the city of Corpus Christi. I did not have to go anywhere looking for it; it came to me. Of course, it was part of God's plan. This is the same job where God revealed to me to go back to school. This is the reason I am attending school at this time. It was not my choice; it is God's plan for my life. It is a beautiful experience when we wait on God and not try to take things in our own hands. I am incredibly grateful I remained in Corpus Christi. My desire has always been wherever God wants me to be. I thank God for His love and how He allowed me to get back on track so I can receive the blessing He has in store for me. This will be a testimony that I can share with others who are waiting on God.

In the book *Lord, Have You Forgotten Me?* Judith Couchman encourages us to hold on to hope. She says the following:

> You Gotta Have Hope
>
> Hope can help us hang on when the future looks bleak and out of control.
>
> Hope thrives best in hard times. The Bible says, "We also exult in our tribulations, knowing that tribulation brings about perseverance; and perseverance, proven character; and proven character, hope; and hope does not disappoint because the love of God has been poured out within our hearts through the Holy Spirit who was given to us" (Romans 5:3–5).
>
> Yet hope isn't something we can conjure up as needed. It's the outflow of God's love in our hearts. And if we're without hope, we can ask Him to renew it, just as He revitalizes the Holy Spirit's work within us. Without hope, people perish. With God's hope, they believe beyond themselves (Couchman, Judith, *Lord, Have You Forgotten Me?* Word Pub. 1992, p. 119).

Joel Osteen speaks on this subject also. He states:

> A Seed of Hope
>
> A seed of hope is the beginning of every good thing in our lives. Hope gives birth to the overcoming life. It always believes for the best, even in the worst circumstances. For believers in Christ,

hope is much more than a wish, yearning, or a positive outlook. It is based on the promises of God found in His Word. They are promises to move on your behalf.

We can have hope in life no matter what surrounds us, because we serve a mighty God who cares, knows us by name (Isaiah 45:3), understands the desires of our heart (1 Chronicles 28:9), and who knew us before we were even formed in our mother's womb (Jeremiah 1:5).

Recently, we all watched the miracle of flight #1549. Instead of ending in a disastrous crash, it gracefully landed on the Hudson River in New York City.

The outcome was nothing short of a miracle. In fact, it is being referred to as "the miracle on the Hudson" because all 152 passengers and all the crew survived.

I thought about the passengers and what must have been racing through their minds in those final minutes before the impact. Amid the cries and prayers, I'm confident there was one thing they all desperately held on to—hope.

Perhaps you are facing setbacks with your job or relationships. Maybe you're struggling financially, or the pressures of life are just overwhelming you. If that's you, there is still hope! God is for you, not against you. His resources are endless, and His power and love know no boundaries. God is on your side. Do not let the enemy, Satan, still your own thoughts, or anyone else tell you anything different. Keep hope alive and never give up (https://www.joelosteen.com 2019)!

HOW PRAYER CAN WALK YOU THROUGH THE STORMS IN YOUR LIFE

Hope is what says it's possible when everything and everyone around you says it's impossible. You keep your hand in the hands of God and continue to press on. You have a goal in mind, and you must be willing to continue.

If you feel you have done all you can do, keep asking God to give you the strength to hold on. Keep your mind on Him; stand on the Word and His promises until He answers. God is faithful, He has not forgotten you, and He is stretching you. Call some of your friends and ask them to stand in prayer with you. Please keep your mind clear so you will be ready and able to hear Him. Do not ever give up on God because He has your best in mind, and the storm will only last as long as He wants it to. You must keep yourself in position, get your candle, listen to some good church music, and sing to the Lord.

In the book *God's Peace for When You Can't Sleep* by Christina Vinson, she shares the following:

> God's Peace for When Your Prayers Aren't Answered
>
> All around you, people are sleeping. The lights in the house next door are out, and even the birds have ceased their singing. But not you. Your mind is full of questions and concerns, worries, and doubts. The reason? Your prayers aren't being answered—at least, not that you see. So instead of sleeping, you're up, pacing the house, wondering why God is seemingly ignoring your requests, trying to make sense of it all. Are you not praying enough? Are you praying too much? Is what you're asking not in His will? Is God testing your faith? There are so many questions, but no answers to speak of, no writing on the wall.
>
> Know that you are not the only one who struggles with wondering why your prayers aren't being answered. We serve a great and mighty

God, but often, His ways are so mysterious and our minds are so futile we get discouraged and frustrated. Does this sound familiar to you?

I urge you, friend—don't give up. Jesus tells us to ask, seek, and knock. And it's important to keep on asking and knocking, even when God seems silent. His silence doesn't mean He isn't listening and working on our behalf, because He is—in ways we can't conceive. There are also times when His answer is wait. Or sometimes the answer is no. These answers make it especially difficult to believe that God really loves us! But we must trust that His "wait" and "no" are because He loves us so much that He has a better answer to situations than what our limited minds can fathom. It's so important to believe and cling to the depths of His love and not get discouraged.

Tonight, even if you aren't necessarily feeling that God is at work in your life, you can be assured that He is indeed working. Scripture tells us our God never sleeps, and that He is faithful to His people. In this very moment, He is carrying out a perfect, heaven-orchestrated story for your life and for the lives of those you love. He's not working in a general way—He's working in an intricate, personalized way. He is near and hears your prayers.

Keep your eyes open for little glimpses of answers and encouragement throughout each day. They'll come. They might not come tonight—but that's okay. Tonight, it's time to rest. Go to sleep reciting God's Word and promises. He will hear every word.

HOW PRAYER CAN WALK YOU THROUGH THE STORMS IN YOUR LIFE

God's Peace for When You Feel Overwhelmed

It's that time of night again. The house is quiet, the stars are shining against the blackened sky, and everyone is asleep. Everyone, that is, except you. Your mind is racing, shoulders still hunched with the day's obligations, fists already clenched with the worries of what a new day will bring. In a word, you're overwhelmed and exhausted.

My friend, take heart. For the burdens you are carrying in your heart, mind, and body aren't yours to bear alone. Again, and again, God reminds us in Scripture that through leaning on Him, we will find rest for our souls—our downtrodden, utterly wearied souls. Jesus Christ Himself doesn't just tell us to give Him our burdens; He offers to take our burdens for us. He commands us, all of us who are weary and heavy laden, to come to Him and lay our burdens down. Not just half of them, not the ones that seem easily fixable—all of them. What He gives in return is like a cooling, soul-satisfying drink: He gives rest.

As you reflect on these words, on the promises and call of the Lord, take in a deep breath. Exhale the stress you are holding, and breathe in the peace of God, letting the promises of His Word flood your tired soul. And then, as you close your eyes and lay your head down, know that He is right there with you: He is your rock, your strength, your ever-present help in times of trouble, even in the quiet hours of the morning. Cling to that rock (Vinson, Christina, *God's Peace for When You Can't Sleep*. Thomas Nelson 2015. pp. 4–5 and 190–191).

6

God Walks with You Through the Valleys

In this article by Whitney Hopler, he shares with us that while walking in the valleys, we can find victory. He writes:

> Life is good on the mountaintops of celebration. But no matter how much we would like to spend our lives up there, we need to walk through the valleys of challenges too. Life is tough in the valleys. Still, there are valuable lessons we can learn in the valleys that we could never learn if we stayed on the mountaintops.
>
> If you find yourself walking through a valley right now, let God teach you as He walks alongside you. Here's how you can find victory in the valleys:
>
> - *The Valley of Uncertainty.* Remember that every day of your life is a gift from God. Thank Him for each day and decide to use your time as well as you can. Don't assume that you have tomorrow; live one day at a time, as best as

you can. Praise God for giving you your life and ask Him to accomplish His full purposes for you. Understand that nothing can take you from Earth until God's plan for you are complete, and nothing can keep you here after God's plan for you are complete.

- *The Valley of Fear.* Know that God wants to use this valley to deepen your faith (http://www.crosswalk.com/faith). Be assured that nothing can change the fact that you belong to God, and He is in ultimate control of your life. Ask God to make you aware of His presence with you and to give you the peace that only He can give—the peace that surpasses all understanding. Remember that God will help you overcome anything that's causing you fear. Ask Him to give you the strength you need. Use your time in this valley to learn how to trust God more, knowing that struggles build trust by showing you how to live out your faith.
- *The Valley of Detours.* Realize that what is a detour to you because it's unexpected is, to God, just part of the expected path for your life. Even though you don't know where the detour will lead, God does. Lift your eyes beyond your circumstances to God and trust Him to guide you well. Cooperate with His plans for you; work with Him instead of against Him. Decide to live your life according to biblical morals and follow God in both adversity and prosperity.

Count on God's promises in Scripture as He works out His plan for your life. Cling to His providence and move forward in confidence.

- *The Valley of Suffering.* Understand that, because God is sovereign, nothing can get to you without first coming through Him. Know that He won't allow you to suffer any more than you can bear, and that the suffering He allows you to experience is all for a good purpose in your life. Ask God to show you what He wants you to learn from your suffering. Use your time of suffering to get to know God better, love Him more, and trust Him more. Don't lose heart; seasons of suffering inevitably end, and often result in positive growth for you.
- *The Valley of Storms.* Invite God to use the storms you go through to stretch your faith. Understand that God can use storms for correcting (returning you to a right relationship with Him), perfecting (to mature you and prepare you for serving more in His kingdom), and instructing (to teach lessons you couldn't learn otherwise). As you struggle through a storm, keep in mind that Jesus is watching and listening, and He is rooting for you. Not only that, but He is praying for you to remain faithful and to learn to trust Him even more. Don't panic, no matter how much rain falls, how loud the thunder crashes, or how close the lightning strikes, because

God is more powerful than any storm you could ever experience.

- *The Valley of Discouragement.* Seek counsel from people who are close to God, rather than from worldly sources. Ask strong Christians to pray for you because their prayers are powerful. Bring your problems and pains to God and ask Him to empower you to handle them according to His will. Ask God for encouragement and know that He will give it to you. Don't isolate yourself or fall into lethargy. Remember that if you wait until you feel like doing something, you often won't do it, but if you decide to take action no matter what your feelings, your feelings will follow. For if you wait to read your Bible (http://www.biblestudytools.com/) until you're in the mood to do so, you probably won't read it. But if you read it anyway, despite your feelings, you'll discover that you'll want to read it more. Trust that obeying God will always bring His blessings into your life. Remember that nothing is impossible for God, and that problems are platforms for Him to work miracles if He chooses to do so. Know that you can do all things through Christ, who strengthens you! Don't quit living a faithful life; if you do, you'll miss out on God's best for you. Be persistent in faith until your circumstances change—and know that, in the process, you will change for the better.

- *The Valley of Confusion.* While walking through this valley, don't let yourself become disoriented. Stay focused on God and firmly cling to Him and His promises, regardless of what happens. He assured that even when your circumstances confuse you, God knows what He's doing in your life. Ask Him to help you trust Him more.
- *The Valley of Correction.* Recognize that every crisis is an opportunity to take a personal inventory to determine how closely you are connected to God. Ask Him to show you any sins in your life that are blocking intimacy with Him. Repent, accept His forgiveness, and embrace the grace He offers to be reconciled with Him. Know that through your repentance, God can restore you and use your life to accomplish great things.
- *The Valley of Sickness.* Understand that sickness is a summons to pray. Don't be shy about praying often, about everything you need, like healing, strength, and wisdom. Intercede for your loved ones and your medical team. Keep praying until answers come. Ask others—especially strong Christians—to pray for you and let them know your specific requests. Don't wait for others to contact you; take the initiative to contact them. Seek the best medical care you can find, pray hard, and never give up hope. Understand that while physical healing isn't guaranteed, God

will intervene according to His will if you pray and he will give you peace and possibly restored health as well (http://www.crosswalk.com/faith/spiritual-life/god-walks-walks-with-you-through-the-valleys-13.)

The Significance of Trials

In the article by Rick James, he shares with us that, sometimes, we run from the trial rather than embracing it and the growth it brings. He states the following:

> I believe that often, trials come into our lives in four thinly veiled disguises that can prevent us from recognizing and embracing their transforming superpower.
>
> In 1 Peter 1:6 and James 1:2, both Peter and James mention, "trials of many kinds." Their point is that trials can be long, short, emotional, physical, mental, or circumstantial and comes with varying degrees of difficulty. Our trials come in all shapes and sizes and do not always come in a spiritual "wrapper."
>
> If you find yourself in some difficult or constraining circumstances that are a source of struggle for you, consider yourself in a trial; it is therefore not random (it was allowed by God) and can work for good in your spiritual growth.
>
> The Disguise of an Obstacle
>
> Most trials seem on the surface to present themselves to us as obstacles that prevent us from living a godly life. Trials are not actually obstacles (though they often feel that way) but are

the fuel for helping us reach our goals. Often, as Christians, when we pray for greater holiness, we find the world caving in around us. Our reactions can make us feel more ungodly than ever.

It is critical to see that while these trials might provide momentary setbacks to our visible progress in the faith, they are ultimately providing the fuel we need to get to our destination. They build our lives, passion, perseverance, and deeper character change that go far beyond the surface behavior change we were trying to manifest in our lives. Often, God answers our prayer for greater holiness, not by proving better circumstances that help us perform better, but by providing trials.

The Disguise of Randomness

In 1 Peter 1:6, it says that "you may have had to suffer grief in all kinds of trials."

The key phrase, "you may have had to," could be translated "it may have become necessary" for you to suffer trials. This verse discloses that there is design and intent behind the trial.

God has looked at your life and decided that it was, in fact, necessary for you to go through a trial for the sake of spiritual growth. Often, Christians fail to persevere in trials, because they begin to believe that they are simply random happenstance and therefore have no point or benefit.

Right now, if you were to go into a hospital and listen in to conversations taking place between friends and family with sick loved ones, you might hear phrases like, "You'll see, it will all work out" or "Every cloud has a silver lining." These people need hope, and loved ones reflexively try to provide it by explaining that their pain has purpose.

Unfortunately, without God, these can be nothing more than shallow platitudes, because there really is no guarantee that their pain will have a positive purpose. However, the Christian always has hope because there is nothing random, unplanned, or unforeseen in any of the trials that come into their lives. For the Christian, absolutely nothing is random. All their pain and trials can have redemptive purposes, and anything that has come into their lives has been allowed by God.

The Disguise of God's Anger

One of the hardest things about trials is that we often think we are experiencing hardship because we have done something wrong, or that God is angry with us. The writer of Hebrews tells us to consider trials as loving discipline from God. He also says that our trials are actually indicators of God's approval, and the reality of our adoption into God's family. God disciplines us—not out of anger—but out of love, and "for our good that we might share in His holiness."

Consider It Joy

In James 1:2, it says, "to consider it pure joy… whenever you face trials of various kinds." Now we have a platform to see how we can consider these insidious obstacles as "pure joy." They have been allowed by God. They are not random. They have specific intent to produce maturity in us, and they are a sign of God's approval and of the legitimacy of our belonging to God's family.

It is also important to note that while we may consider trials to be a blessing, it does not mean we must always feel emotionally happy as we endure them. Sometimes, Christians can be successful in their handling of trials—enduring them—yet feel like a failure because they don't feel overly happy.

Knowing you are blessed can make you feel happy, but not always. Joy is a state of "contentment," even freedom, within constraining circumstances. We can experience this within the course of a trial when we see that it has been allowed by God, is for our good, and is a sign of God's approval of us.

How Do Trials Actually Change Me?

First Peter 1:6–7 is one of the most valuable passages on trials, because it describes the dynamics of how God changes us within the context of a trial. Peter describes the gold smelting process where gold is heated up and impurities float to the surface. The next step in the process is to scoop away the dross, or impurities. The result is a purer piece of gold.

The result, then, of trials (the heating up of our lives) is to accomplish a purer and stronger character and faith. It is in the "heating up" of our lives that our weaknesses, sin, and character flaws come to the surface, so that they may be transformed.

As the heat brings impurities of character to the surface, it also raises issues of deficiency in our faith. For example, in a trial, we might begin to believe that God doesn't love us, that He is angry with us, or that our suffering has no purpose. As a result, we begin to cling in our hearts to the truth of God's character presented in Scripture. When we come through the trial, we find that our faith has been stretched to several times its original size, as we own the character of God in a way we never did before.

Like the growth of a muscle lifting weights, the resistance of the trial causes the muscle of faith to grow stronger.

In the heat of trials is where these deficiencies in faith and character surface. It is only when they surface that God can begin to purify our hearts, motives, and actions.

Why Do I Need Trials?

Trials produce maturity, and this is why they are a blessing to us. James 1:4 describes a progression where trials produce perseverance, and perseverance, maturity. The goal of trials is not to make a person more persevering. That's not a very exciting goal, but the result of persevering under trials is a mature character and faith. This is motivating. All Christians want the fruit of maturity, godly character, and faith (https://www.cru.org/us/en/blog/life-and-relationships/hardships/the-significance-of-trials. 1994-2019 Cru).

In the book *How to Let God Solve Your Problems*, Charles Stanley tells us adversity is a time for self-examination. He states the following:

To Provide an Opportunity for Self-Examination

The winds of adversity reveal the real person you are inside. When life is going well, you will never stop to think if there is anything wrong with what you are doing. Most people think that if life is going along smoothly, then God must be pleased with them. However, when the bottom drops out of life and problems begin to appear, we are much more likely to stop and pray, "Lord, show me if there is anything within me that is not pleasing to You." God allows the winds of adversity to blow long enough and strong enough until we are driven to examine what we are doing.

When you feel buffeted by adversity, one of the most natural things for you to do is to examine your heart to see if you are right before the Lord. "God, am I in Your will, or have I taken a step in the wrong direction? If the problem is not the result of sin, then are You trying to show me something?" God deals with root attitudes buried deep inside of us. Many of these have been in our lives since we were young. Those predetermined, preprogrammed attitudes often deal with our self-esteem and attitudes toward others. We may confess the problem and admit the sin, but this will not take care of it. God wants to change us so that our lives reflect His grace and mercy to others. He begins the process of sweeping our hearts clean.

If you respond to the situation and God the right way, He will reveal where you have taken a wrong turn. Or if the problem has come as a natural result of life's sorrows and trials, He will give you the strength and wisdom you need to get through the difficulty.

HOW PRAYER CAN WALK YOU THROUGH THE STORMS IN YOUR LIFE

Regardless of the reason, the moment you cry out to God with an open and willing heart, He moves to comfort, encourage, and guide you. Remember, the intensity of His adversity is always limited to your capacity to bear it. He will never send adversity into your life and break your spirit. He will never use trouble or heartache to destroy you. He may use these to gain your love and attention, but in doing so, He is always working behind the scenes to build you up and bring you to a point where your life can be used for His maximum potential. Adversity is a tool God may use to shape your life. It can be a great source for spiritual growth or a point of discouragement. It all depends on how you allow Him to work in your life.

The key to overcoming problems is in our response to difficulties. God knows that heartache and disappointment are hard to bear. But He reminds us in Romans 8:28 that He would work all things together for our good and His glory. This means that even when we refuse to obey Him, once we have confessed our disobedience and asked Him to forgive us, He will do just that and also will restore our fellowship with Him.

If we are going through a dark time, when problems are stacked on every side, then you know that God is on the move in your life, and He has a great reward waiting for you when you yield your heart and life to Him (Stanley, Charles F., *How to Let God Solve Your Problems: 12 keys for finding clear guidance in life's trials*. Thomas Nelson 2008 88–89).

In the book by Charles Stanley, *How to Handle Adversity*, Charles Stanley encourages us to learn how to respond correctly to adversity, and by doing so, we work with God instead of against Him. He shares the following:

The Choice Is Yours

The nature of our adversity alone does not determine its spiritual value in our lives. It is our reaction to it, the way we deal with it, that makes suffering valuable. We have all seen people who faced tough times and folded under pressure. Some pull themselves back together and go on to learn whatever God wants to teach them. Others never recuperate.

The Blame Game

When adversity strikes, our first response oftentimes is to blame somebody. I can remember standing at the scene of an automobile accident, listening to a college student trying to explain to the police officer why he had turned in front of a lady. He was sure that it was not his fault; something about the angle of the traffic light threw him off. He was clearly to blame. But this young man was so angry at having wrecked his car; he could not stand the thought of it being his fault.

We all have a tendency to strike out at those around us when things go wrong, or we are hurt. Remember Mary and Martha's response: "Lord, if You had been here…" Some people blame God. Others blame Satan. But usually, we pin the blame on another person in attempt to escape personal responsibility.

If blaming it on someone else does not get us anywhere, we may find ourselves fighting the problem. We attempt to manipulate or reshape our circumstances so, as to rid ourselves of pain and inconvenience. This is the reason behind many lawsuits. People who have been fired or passed by for a promotion may sue the company. They feel compelled to fight for their rights.

Another way people react to tragedy is denial. They simply will not face what has happened. They act as if nothing is wrong. I see this in situations in which someone has lost a loved one. And a parent or a friend refuses to accept the separation as permanent. This is usually a temporary situation. In time, most of these people are able to accept what has happened.

Any of the preceding responses can easily turn into bitterness—bitterness toward the person or organization through which adversity comes or even bitterness toward God. When people become bitter, the very thought of the person who hurt them causes their stomach to turn. Bitterness forces people to overreact to circumstances that remind them of those times when they were wronged.

At this stage, people may think about revenge. All of us are guilty at one time or another of rehearsing in our minds what we would like to do to somebody if we thought we could get away with it. We imagine ourselves walking into the office of our boss and letting him have it. Or perhaps calling our parents and telling them just what we think. Whatever the case, whenever there is a routine of imaginary confrontation, that is a good indication that bitterness has set in.

Bitterness toward God is much the same. A person who is bitter toward God cannot discuss religion objectively. There is always emotion involved.

The Pity Party

Another common way of dealing with adversity is self-pity. Individuals suffering from self-pity have drawn an imaginary circle around themselves and their circumstances.

The only people they will allow in are those who want to join them in their misery.

Consequently, they do oftentimes end up alone. No one wants to be around that type of person for long. This solitude serves to reinforce their negative perspective, and they cling to it tightly.

It is not unusual for these people to become depressed. Hopelessness overwhelms them, and they see no reason for going on with life. Depressed persons are unable to interpret accurately the events around them. Thus, if left alone, they tend to get worse.

Responding the wrong way to adversity will always have a devastating effect. People who react in any of the ways just described will always come out the losers. It is understandable why those who hurt react the way they do. But regardless of how understandable their response may be, if it is a wrong response, they will suffer just the same.

Holding on to anger and bitterness is always self-destructive, both are poisonous. They poison your relationships, your decision-making ability, and your testimony. You cannot carry anger and bitterness and emerge from adversity as a winner.

Responding incorrectly to adversity only prolongs the agony. This is especially true if there is something specific God wants to teach you. He will not let up until He has accomplished His will.

God wants to use our pain and sorrow for something positive. When we respond incorrectly, we can rest assured He will devise another way to give us a second or third chance to handle it right.

The Right Response—The Wages of Sin

Sin always results in adversity of some form. Some types are certainly more obvious than others. And some are more devastating in their effect. But there is always a consequence of some sort, even if it is only guilt. The following are some steps I have found helpful in dealing with the consequences of sin:

1. *Assume the responsibility.* Don't look for someone to blame. Don't think about what would have happened if someone had done something differently? Take the responsibility; own up to it. Admit to yourself that you are facing adverse circumstances because of your own doing.

2. *Confess and repent of your sin.* To confess is to agree with God. Tell God you have sinned. Not that you have made a mistake. Not that you have had an accident. Simply agree with Him that it is sin. Then repent of your sin. Make a decision not to return to it. That may entail ending a relationship. It may mean

leaving your place of employment. You may have to go back to people you have wronged and apologize. Perhaps you have stolen from someone. Repentance would involve returning what you have taken. To repent is to make every arrangement necessary not to go back to the same sin. That way God knows you are serious.

3. *Do not complain.* If you are suffering because of something you have done, you have no right to complain. You brought this on yourself. Don't spend your time trying to gain people's sympathy. Use your energy to get things right with God.

4. *Ask God to help you discover the weakness through which sin crept into your life.* Is this a flaw in your thinking? Have you adopted ideas into your philosophy of life that are contrary to Scripture? Do you have an area of insecurity you have never dealt with? Do you have friends who drag you down? Is there someone in your life who is a constant source of temptation? Questions like these can help you pinpoint the door through which sin has entered and found a resting place in your life.

5. *Recognize that God wants to use this adversity in your life.* Regardless of the source, adversity is always a tool when entrusted to the hands of the Lord. Tell Him, "Lord, I know that I am suffering because of my own doing. But I trust that You will use this time of adversity to deepen my faith and strengthen my commitment to You."

6. *Thank God for not allowing you to get by with your sin.* True repentance is followed by genuine gratitude. When you see your sin for what it is, and if you believe God disciplines those He loves, it makes sense to thank Him for sending adversity into your life.

Adversity from Above and Below

Responding to adversity when it originates with God or Satan is different from merely responding to the consequences of sin. Yet the way you respond when God is behind it and the way you respond when Satan is behind it is identical. This may come as a surprise. But think about it. Most of the time, you really do not know who is behind it. And it really does not matter. What is important is your response.

Beyond that, however, another principle becomes a factor. You know that if God is behind it, He is going to use it for your good. If Satan is behind it, he is going to use it for God's supervision. As you have seen in the life of Paul, God uses even Satan's schemes to accomplish His will. You are not pressed to discover the source, but you are expected to respond correctly.

You may think, *shouldn't I resist the devil? Shouldn't I stand against him with Scripture and prayer?* Absolutely—when he comes at you with temptation. For you know that God has no part in tempting you. But we are not talking temptation. The focus is adversity, unexpected tragedy, and suffering. When these things occur, and you are sure it is not the direct result of your sin, here is how you should respond:

1. *Reaffirm your position in Christ.* Remind yourself of who you are and what you have in Christ. It helps to do it aloud. You can say something like this:

    I know that I am a child of God. I am saved. I have been placed into Christ. I am sealed with the Holy Spirit. My eternal destiny is determined, and nothing can change that. The Lord will never leave me or forsake me. The angel of the Lord encampeth round about me. Nothing can touch me apart from what my loving Father allows. All things will work together for my good since I love God and have been called according to His purpose in Christ Jesus.

2. *Ask God to remove the adversity from your life.* This is usually where we begin. And I am sure the Lord understands. But it is best to ask after we have regained some perspective. Paul asked that his adversity be removed. God did not chastise him for that request, nor will he be displeased with your request.

3. *Reaffirm the promise of God's sustaining grace.* As we have seen, God may choose not to remove adversity from your life immediately. When that is the case, it is imperative that you rely on His grace rather than your own strength. People who try to endure suffering in their own strength go down under the weight of it all. Admit that you do not have the power to withstand the pressure. Cry out to God for mercy. He will hear you; His grace will be sufficient moment by moment to get you through.

4. *Thank God for this unique opportunity to grow spiritually.* You must look for God's part in your adversity, or you will miss it. You are not simply to endure suffering; you are to grow and mature through it. From the beginning, you must look for the lessons God wants to teach you. The best way to develop this attitude is to thank Him every day for the spiritual growth He is bringing about in your life.

5. *Receive adversity as if it were from God.* It does not matter if the adversity you are facing originated with Satan. Receive it as if it were from God. You know that nothing can happen to you unless He allows it. And if He allows it, He must certainly have a purpose in it. Therefore, as long as God is accomplishing His purpose through the adversity in your life, you can receive it as if it were from Him. When you respond to adversity as if it were from Satan, the tendency is to fight it. When it lingers, you may begin to doubt God. I learned this principle during one of the most difficult periods of my life.

   After being at First Baptist Church for only a year, several deacons began a move to get me out of the church. As I prayed, I knew beyond any doubt that God wanted me to stay. Things got rough for a while. People whom I thought were my friends turned on me. I never knew where I stood from week to week.

   On the one hand, I knew that if God wanted me to stay at FBC and they wanted me to leave, they certainly were not being led of the Spirit. That left only one option.

Satan was clearly behind the controversy. Yet on the other hand, I knew that somehow the Lord was in it as well. One day, I was in my office praying, and a thought came to me that I know now was from the Lord: The only way to deal with this is not to look at men, but to keep your eyes on Me. It doesn't matter who says what, when, where, or how. You must see all this as coming from Me.

From that moment on, I begin thanking God for what He was doing. Things got worse before they got better. But God was faithful. He accomplished many great things through that time—both in my life and in the life of the church. In spite of all the rejection and deception, I never grew bitter. To this day, I am not resentful. The thing that got me through it was trusting that somehow God was in it and that when He had accomplished His purpose, things would change. In the meantime, my responsibility was to remain faithful.

As long as you are able to believe that God is involved in the adversity you are facing, you will have hope. Regardless of who initiated it, God is in it! And if He is in it, His grace for you will be sufficient. It does not make any difference who the source is. It matters little who the messenger is. As long as you respond as if it were from God, you will come out a winner.

6. *Read and meditate on Scripture describing the adversities of God's servants.* Read the story of Joseph. Put yourself in the place of Moses when he was told he could not enter the Promised Land. Look at the way God pro-

vided for Abraham when he was left with the least desirable land. Imagine how foolish Noah felt while building the ark. The Bible contains illustration after illustration of God's faithfulness in adverse circumstances. Fill your mind with these truths. Ask Him to open your eyes to the human side of these characters that you might be able to identify with their pain and their sorrow. Then dwell on Christ's promise to care for those who love Him (see Matthew 6:25–34). Just as He was faithful to those whose stories are in the old and New Testaments, so will He demonstrate His faithfulness to you.

A Final Word

Suffering is unavoidable. It comes without a warning; it takes us by surprise. It can shatter or strengthen us. It can be the source of great bitterness or abounding joy. It can be the means by which our faith is destroyed. Or it can be the tool through which our faith is deepened. The outcome hinges not on nature or source of our adversity, but on the character and spirit of our response. Our response to adversity will, for the most part, be determined by our reason for living, our purpose for being on this Earth, as we see it.

If you are a child of God whose heart's desire is to see God glorified through you, adversity will not put you down for the count. There will be those initial moments of shock and confusion. But the man or woman who has God's perspective on this life and the life to come will always emerge victorious (Stanley, Charles, *How to Handle Adversity?* Thomas Nelson, 2008, pp. 171–181.)

7

Wisdom in the Midst of Trials

Charles Stanley tells us that we need wisdom to learn from God as we walk through our hardship and pain. He writes the following in his article:

> We need wisdom to discern the source of our trials.
>
> The origin of suffering is not always obvious. It could be sent by God for His purposes, but Satan also tries to thwart us with trouble and pain. Sometimes, we're simply reaping the consequences of our foolish choices, or suffering as a result of someone else's actions. At other times, the difficulty appears to happen accidentally, and no one is responsible.
>
> No matter what the source, the Lord is always sensitive to our pain. Furthermore, we are surrounded by His awesome, divine protection. As God's children, nothing touches us unless it first passes through His sovereign and loving

hands. Everything He allows in our lives has the potential of being beneficial to us. His goal is not to harm but to bless.

We need wisdom to discern the purpose of our trials.

The Lord uses suffering to accomplish His will in our lives. When we cooperate with His plans, not only are we benefited, but we're able to bless other people as well. Furthermore, when we understand what He's trying to accomplish, we're able to rejoice even in our pain.

When we fail to understand God's purposes for our trials:

- We'll see them only as negative, senseless events having no connection to God.
- We won't understand the Lord's ways, and as a result, our pain will seem pointless.
- We'll miss the blessing God wanted to give us.
- We will feel defeated, hopeless, and helpless.
- We'll be disappointed because of our inability to handle difficult situations in our own strength.
- We will see ourselves as victims of our circumstances rather than recipients of the Lord's protective care.
- We'll feel controlled by other people instead of recognizing ultimate control.

We need wisdom to discern the proper response to our trials.

If we believe all that Scriptures say about the benefits available to us in difficulties and pain, we will stop moaning and groaning, and instead, rejoice that God is up to something in our lives. We will never be able to rejoice in the midst of pain and suffering:
- If our priorities aren't right, we won't seek wisdom.
- If we value comfort more than what God is doing in our character, trials will upset us.
- If we value the material and physical more than the spiritual, we can't count it all joy when we experience hardship.
- If we live only for the present and forget the future, our difficulties will make us bitter instead of better (https://www.intouch.org 2015).

This is why each day is a new beginning; God allows us to repent of our sins and start fresh every day. He knows we can't manage this life on our own; this is the reason He provides us with everything we need. We must be willing to use His tools so they can bless us. We have access to tap into His benefits, as His children. God wants us to be successful in our storms, and He knows how much pain we can take, so He will never put more than we can handle on us. Sometimes, it may seem more than we can handle, but trust God; He knows what He is doing.

In the book, *Walking Wisely*, Charles Stanley shares the following:

HOW PRAYER CAN WALK YOU THROUGH THE STORMS IN YOUR LIFE

The Foundation for Walking Wisely

Proverbs 9:10 tells us, "The fear of the Lord is the beginning of wisdom." "Fear" in this verse refers to reverence for God. Those who fear God stand in awe of God. They have at least a glimmer of understanding that God is omniscient (all-wise), omnipotent (all-powerful), omnipresent (present in every moment and throughout all eternity), and all-loving, and that they are not. They stand before God in wonderment and amazement that God, who is all, has all, and controls all, cares, loves, reaches out, and blesses the individual human being. To fear God is not to fear God's judgment; it is to stand in awe that God has all authority to judge and to forgive, to show mercy, and to grant His grace in overflowing abundance.

Spiritual wisdom is given to those who accept Jesus Christ as their Savior, commit themselves to following God in obedience, seek to develop a relationship with Him, reverence Him, and walk out their days submitted to, yielded to, and listening to the Holy Spirit.

Are you wiser than God, who made human nature, when it comes to knowing how to develop and maintain good relationships?

Who would be so foolish as to say he or she is wiser than the Creator and sovereign King of this universe? How ridiculously arrogant to say in the face of God, "I know more than You do. I know better than You know. I have a better idea than Your idea" (Stanley, Charles, *Walking Wisely*. Thorndike Press, 2005, pp. 16–17).

8

The Holy Spirit

Joyce Meyer shares with us the purpose of the Holy Spirit in our lives. She indicates the following:

The Divine Helper

There are countless things that we struggle with when we could be receiving help from the Divine Helper. The Holy Spirit is a Gentleman; He will not push His way into our life or our daily affairs. If given an invitation, He is quick to respond, but He must be invited.

As the third person of the Trinity, the Holy Spirit has a personality. He can be offended and grieved. He must be treated with great respect. Once we have the understanding that He lives inside those of us who believe, we should do everything we can to make Him feel at home.

The Holy Spirit is always available. The Amplified Bible calls Him the Standby. I love that particular trait because I like to think of Him just standing by me all the time in case I need help with anything at all. Just think about that for a while, and it gets pretty exciting. One of the most powerful prayers we can pray is, "Lord, help me!"

Not only is the Holy Spirit standing by to help in any situation that requires it, He is also available for counsel. How often do we run to our friends when we should be asking the Holy Spirit for advice? He desires to lead, guide, and direct our lives; it honors Him when we ask for His advice.

I feel honored when my grown children ask for my advice, and I especially feel honored when they take it. I always have the best interest in mind and would never tell them anything if I did not firmly believe it would help them. If we as humans can do that, how much more can the Holy Spirit do for us if we will turn to Him?

I think many people never find answers to their problems because they seek out wrong sources for advice and counsel.

How does the Holy Spirit counsel us?

One of the greatest ways that God leads His people is through the inner witness. In other words, we just know inside what is right or what is wrong. It is a deeper level of knowing than head knowledge. This type of knowing is in the spirit—we simply have peace or a lack of peace, and by that peace or lack of it, we know what we should do.

I once talked with a woman who needed to make a serious decision. Her family and friends were giving her advice, but she needed to know within herself what the right answer was because she was the one who would have to live with it. She had been in a certain business all of her life and was feeling that she wanted to get out of it and stay home with her children. Of course, this would mean severe financial changes as well as personal changes for her that might affect her emotionally. She needed to know from a Higher Source than other people what the right thing was for her to do.

This woman went to a retreat with a relative. Sometime during the course of that weekend, as she sat praising and worshipping the Lord and listening to the speaker, a knowing and peace came into her heart that she was indeed right in closing the business. She said a moment came when she simply knew what was right. Ever since that time, she has had peace about it.

It is amazing how many people can tell us things that have no effect upon us, but when God tells us something, we feel totally different. Other people cannot always give us peace with their advice, but God can.

The Holy Spirit comforts us

The Holy Spirit also wants to help us by comforting us when we need it. You and I may need to be comforted when we have been disappointed, hurt, or mistreated in some way or when we have experienced loss. We may also need to be comforted during changes in our life or even when we are just simply tired.

God will not only allow people to do a certain amount and no more for us. Even those people who are extremely close to us cannot give us everything we need all the time. When we expect others to do for us what only God can do, we have our expectations in the wrong place, and we will always be disappointed.

There is no comfort that is as good as God's. Man can never give us what we really need, unless God Himself uses other people to reach us, which He often does.

The Holy Spirit strengthens us

The Holy Spirit also offers His help as our Strengthener. Just imagine having a well of strength inside you, a source you can draw on anytime you feel the need. When you feel week or tired or discouraged to that point of giving up, just stop for a few minutes. Close your eyes, if possible, and ask the Holy Spirit to strengthen you. As you wait in His presence, you can often actually feel the strength of God coming to you.

Start receiving the strength of God by faith. It will quicken your body as well as your spirit and soul. For example, if you have a weak back, it can be made strong. At our conferences, the Holy Spirit has strengthened weak knees, ankles, and backs as we have prayed for those who waited in His presence and received it from Him.

By faith you can receive strength to stay in a difficult marriage, raise a difficult child, or stick with a difficult job in which you have a difficult boss. You can receive strength to do great things even though you may have physical impairment yourself.

The strength of God really is amazing. David wrote in Psalm 18:29 "that by his God he could run through a troop and leap over a wall." First Kings 19:4–8, "An angel came and ministered to Elijah who was tired and depressed, and he went forty days and nights in the strength that he received from that one visit."

The Holy Spirit is our intercessor

Why can't we just intercede ourselves? Why do we need the Holy Spirit to help us in this area? The answer is found in 1 Corinthians 2:11, "For what a person perceives [knows and understands] what passes through a man's thoughts except the man's own spirit within him? Just so no one discerns [comes to know and comprehend] the thoughts of God except the Spirit of God." We need the help of the Holy Spirit because He is the only One who accurately knows the thoughts of God.

If you and I are to pray in the will of God, we must know what God is thinking and what He desires. Romans 8:26–28 tells us that we don't know how to pray as we should, so the Holy Spirt helps us.

If we pray by the Holy Spirit, we can always be assured that all things will work out for good. God is great and mighty; there is no situation that He cannot use for good as we pray and trust Him.

The Holy Spirit is our advocate

In *Vine's Complete Expository Dictionary of Old and New Testament Words*, the Greek word *parakletos*, translated *advocate*, is defined under the heading COMFORTER. According to Vine, it means "'called to one's side,' i.e., to one's aid."

The Holy Spirit is One who is literally called to our side to give us aid in every way. When we need defense, He defends us, acting as a legal assistance would for a client. It is good to know that we don't have to defend ourselves when we are accused of something; we can ask for help from the Holy One and expect to receive it. He is our Advocate. That should bring us comfort just thinking about it (Meyer, Joyce, *Knowing God Intimately: being as close to Him as you want to be.* Faith Words 2015, 88–98).

The Nine Fruits of the Holy Spirit

Michael Bradley shares with us that God wants to transmit and impart nine specific fruits of the Holy Spirit into our personalities. He tells us the following:

> God wants all of us to enter into a true sanctification process with Him so that He can begin the process of molding, shaping, and transforming us into the express image of His Son, Jesus Christ. He wants to make us into a better and more holy people. He wants to transform us by the renewing of our minds. He wants to put right thinking into our thought process.
>
> Your job will be to get into the Word to find out exactly what it is God wants to change about you. You will need to find out what godly qualities God will want you to try and "put on" into your personality and what qualities He will want you to try and "put away."
>
> Here is a list of the fruit of the Holy Spirit, which is found in Galatians 5: 22.
>
> 1. Love
> 2. Joy
> 3. Peace
> 4. Longsuffering

5. Kindness
6. Goodness
7. Faithfulness
8. Gentleness
9. Self-control (https://www.bible-knowledge.com/fruits-of-the-holy-spirit/)

Here is a brief example describing the Fruit of the Spirit.

1. *Love.* I am loving you unconditionally, and I do not expect anything in return.
2. *Joy.* Delight ourselves in the Lord, and we can have joy even in the midst of our circumstances because we know who He is.
3. *Peace.* We can rest and have assurance in the Savior and know that we can sleep like a baby. The peace that surpasses all understanding. It removes the anxiety and worries.
4. *Patience.* It is having the desire to wait, because I know God has something special for me. It is standing in the midst of my pain and waiting on God to answer.
5. *Kindness.* It is showing others how much we care for them or showing compassion for someone.
6. *Goodness.* It is being honest, having integrity. It is doing the right thing even when no one is looking.
7. *Faithfulness.* When you tell someone you are going to do something, you stick to your word. This is a person who is loyal to you.
8. *Gentleness.* This is someone who is slow to speak, but when the person speaks, other people listen.
9. *Self-Control.* You can make a decision on what is important rather than on what is urgent.

Please take the time to go through this list and see what fruit you already have in your life. You can make an entry in your journal and thank God for the fruit you have.

HOW PRAYER CAN WALK YOU THROUGH
THE STORMS IN YOUR LIFE

This is also an opportunity to seek the fruit you do not have. The fruit of the Spirit is evidence that our character is becoming more like Jesus.

What Is Faith?

So what is faith? According to *Merriam-Webster's Learner's Dictionary*, faith is defined as "a strong belief or trust in someone or something; belief in the existence of God; strong religious feeling or belief; a system of religious beliefs." Faith is an essential part of a man's relationship with God and is a prerequisite to beginning the conversation process with Christ. For "without faith we cannot please God" (Hebrews 11:6). Essentially, if a person does not believe in Him, he will not have a desire to please Him (learnersdictionary.com).

In the book, *Be Anxious for Nothing*, Joyce Meyer speaks on the same subject.

She shares with us that according to Colossians 1:4, faith is the leaning of your entire human personality on God in absolute trust and confidence in His power, wisdom, and goodness.

This means we need to lean all of ourselves on God, believing only He has the ability to do for us what needs to be done in us. Our only job is to abide in Him, to lean on Him totally and completely, to put our trust and confidence in Him (Meyer, Joyce. *Be Anxious for Nothing: the art of casting your cares and resting in God*. Faith Words 2017, p. 48).

Jack Wellman, in this article, discusses "mustard seed" faith, its meaning, and application in life. He writes:

HOW PRAYER CAN WALK YOU THROUGH THE STORMS IN YOUR LIFE

What did Jesus mean when He said if you have little faith as a mustard seed? Does this mean that we only need a small amount of faith? Can tiny amounts of faith really move mountains? What is the meaning of this saying of Jesus and the applications for our life?

The Mustard Seed

Mustard trees have been found in various locations throughout the world. Even though it's one of the smallest seeds, the trees can grow up to 20 feet tall and 20 feet wide. The tree can grow in arid, dry climates and thrive even in clay or sandy soil. It can grow in hot, dry weather or cool, wet climates. I see the mustard seed as being symbolic of faith in that our faith can be tested in the "dry times," the most difficult of circumstances (drought, poor soil, and in clay or sandy ground). Also, even if the tree is cut down to the trunk, it can grow back again, so the analogy is that even during times of pruning, the believer can overcome and come back stronger than ever, just like the mustard tree that's been severely pruned and even if only a tiny bit of faith remains. The mustard tree is drought tolerant, and if we have faith even the size of a tiny mustard seed, we too can tolerate the dry times in our lives, the difficult growing seasons of a Christian, and even when we are "planted" in poor soil, we can still grow, even if we only have a small amount of faith. Incidentally, the mustard tree has many uses. The leaves can be made into, you guessed it, mustard. The tree can produce edible salts, some have used the small branches as toothbrushes, the leaves have been shown to prevent tooth decay and alleviate toothaches. The implications of this tree are not lost in a dead and decaying world.

The Seed of Faith

There are many scriptures that Jesus used about the mustard seed. In Matthew 17:20, Jesus said, "Because you have so little faith. Truly I tell you, if you have faith like a grain of a mustard seed, you can say to the mountain, 'Move from here to there,' and it will move. Nothing will be impossible for you."

Jesus compared the mustard seed to the Kingdom, saying, "The kingdom of heaven is like a mustard seed, which a man took and planted in his field" (Matthew 13:31), and "If you have faith as small as a mustard seed, you can say to this mulberry tree, 'Be uprooted and planted in the sea,' and it will obey you" (Luke 17:6). Jesus seems to be saying that the Kingdom of God, at the time of Jesus's earthly ministry, was small in the beginning and from this tiny seed, it would grow and grow. Would this growth ever stop? No, as Isaiah wrote, "Of the greatness of his government and peace there will be no end. He will reign on David's throne and over his kingdom, stabling and upholding it with justice and righteousness from that time on and forever. The zeal of the LORD Almighty will accomplish this" (Isaiah 9:7). This tiny "seed" would never stop growing and when the King of this Kingdom comes to rule in power on Earth, it will apparently continue to grow forever and ever. It appears that this Kingdom will expand for all eternity and perhaps into the entire universe…all from one of the tiniest (most humble) of beginnings

HOW PRAYER CAN WALK YOU THROUGH THE STORMS IN YOUR LIFE

(https://www.whatchristianswantstoknow.com/mustard-seed-faith-meaning-and-life-lessons).

The following article also addresses the topic of mustard seed faith. It states:

> The mustard seed is a striking example of a potential of a seed. Although it starts out small and insignificant, it quickly grows into something that blesses others.
>
> A seed does nothing until it is planted. Jesus seems to indicate that our faith is planted by speaking. "If you have faith as a mustard seed, you will say…"
>
> So to have mustard seed faith, we have to say something. Saying what God says in His Word is our best choice. A seed can even push aside rocks or other obstacles, but it does not do so instantaneously. A seed does not move hindrances by an explosive burst, but by a relentless expansion of growth continually pushing outward and upward.
>
> As a seed becomes a plant, it continues to draw nutrients from its source, and thus continues to grow bigger and stronger forcing hindrances out of its way. No seed is ever affected by what other seeds do. Even if other seeds die, it keeps on.
>
> A seed is persistent, never giving up. Only death stops it from growing and working to produce fruit. This may be the most important characteristic of a mustard seed: it never gives up ("Mustard Seed Faith." www.adevotion.org/archive/mustard-seed-faith/2016/10/8).

Faith is a growing process. We have to trust God just a little bit and see what He can do for us. Once we can see a portion of what He can do, we will begin to trust Him a little more. When we learn how to practice a little bit of faith, it will continue to grow; the more we practice, the more it becomes a habit. I recall a growing point in my life where I had no choice but to trust God. I was living away from my family, no job; who could I turn to but God? Sometimes, God allows us to experience these types of situations so we can grow closer to Him and learn how to trust Him so our faith can increase.

At this point in my life, I decided to pray, fast, and allow God to work in my life. I made up my mind over the weekend that I would begin to fast the following Monday. I asked God to allow someone to call me for a job. I felt like I had looked everywhere I could think of and sent resume after resume; every answer was, "You are overqualified," or "We are still interviewing other candidates." I told God, I was going to let Him do whatever He wanted with me because my life belongs to Him. I already knew to keep praying no matter what happens in my life. I have always kept the word PUSH in my mind, which stands for "pray until something happens."

I began to put messages on my bathroom mirrors to remind me to keep trusting God and praying for someone to call me. God allowed my phone to ring a little before twelve noon. A young lady that I had spoken with over the phone called to tell me there is a job opening in a nursing home. I told her I would send my resume to them. I immediately sent my resume to this company, and I received a call from them the same day.

When they called me, they asked if I could come to Dallas for an interview. I explained to them that I had been out of a job for a couple of months and did not have the funds to purchase a plane ticket, but I was willing to drive to Dallas for the interview. They asked me to call the airport and schedule a flight for this afternoon and call them back with the reservation number so they could pay for the ticket. I made the arrangements, called them back, and gave them the information. My neighbor took me to the airport, and the company had someone to pick me up from the airport and transport me to their office. This company paid for my hotel stay, took me out to dinner, and gave me some spending money. I was offered the job before I left Dallas the next day.

This is how God works; I trusted Him because I knew only He could give me what I needed. This increased my faith and allowed me to trust Him more. He walked with me through my storm. I put my hand in His hand and allowed Him to work in my life. When I think of this experience, all I can say is it was God taking care of me; that is what He does for His children. He provides, we ask, He gives, and we praise Him and be grateful. He is waiting to help us.

In my life, when it appears as if He is not working, He works all night long while I am asleep. When I do not see the progress, I focus on the words of the *Footprints in the Sand*. "When you saw only one set of footprints, it was then that I carried you." When I think about God carrying me through the tough things and giving me the encouragement I need, this is a beautiful experience. I can put my head on His shoulder and just relax and have peace as I continue in the storm. He certainly gives me great assurance as I walk and talk with Him throughout my life. I can never ask for a better father than Him.

Over the years, I can certainly see how my faith has increased, but I have a long way to go. I recall, as a younger sister in Christ, telling God I wanted to become a woman of faith. I began reading books on faith and trying to learn what I could about it. My favorite verses in the Bible are Hebrews 11:1 and Hebrew 11:6 KJV which say the following:

> Now faith is the substance of things hoped for, the evidence of things not seen. (Hebrews 11:1)
>
> But without faith it is impossible to please him: for he that cometh to God must believe that he is, and that he is a rewarder of them that diligently seek him. (Hebrews 11:6)

These verses have helped me to get through some rough moments in my life. I like repeating the scriptures several times throughout the day, writing a scripture on a piece of paper and placing it in my shoe and walking on it all day long. I keep telling myself I have the faith, I need to trust God to work in my life, and I am going to stay strong throughout this storm.

Keeping Faith in Hard Times

In this article, Jenn Johns explains how one has to choose to trust God, not only in times of peace but in times of difficulty also. She writes:

> Going by faith—or, really living by faith—is about the free-will choice to trust God and choose His way over our own.
>
> And it is about keeping that faith, not just in times of peace, but in times when life feels grindy. In times when we want to give up or choose another path.
>
> I'd love to say I get this right all the time, but I don't. I want to.
>
> In fact, just after writing two blog posts about living by faith and genuinely desiring it in my life, I felt riddled with jabbing trials and temptations.
>
> In each situation, it seemed like I could see the problem clear enough to choose otherwise. I could see there was a way out, but then temptation blew in over and over.
>
> It whispered all the thoughts my "self" wanted to hear. Words like "just give up," "feel bad" or "who needs that crap." (Sorry—that's how temptation sounds in my ear at times.)
>
> And why are these defeating thoughts even tempting? Maybe because it feels like "someone understands"—Yes, right, just give up; I totally should!

But who is the "someone who understands?" Would God draw near in a trying time and whisper, "Just give up" (http://goingbyfaith.com/keeping-faith-in-trials-temptations-and-tough-times/)?

Learning to Live by Faith

In the article, "Learning to Live by Faith," Joyce Meyer tells us how to release our faith. She begins by saying:

> It's one thing to believe in Jesus as your Savior and exercise your faith for salvation, but there are many things for which we need to release our faith after we're born again. Faith doesn't end with our salvation; from that point, God wants us to live by faith.
>
> It's so important to get a revelation about this. For many years, I didn't understand what it meant to live by faith. As a result, I didn't have real peace and joy in my life. But once I decided to go deeper in my relationship with God, I learned that I can exercise my faith in Him for the things I need. Philippians 4:6 says, "Don't worry about anything; instead, pray about everything. Tell God what you need, and thank Him for all He has done" (NLT).
>
> Faith can grow, but it only grows when we use it. It's like a muscle. The way you build a bigger muscle is through effort—you have to use it. As it grows, you have to use heavier weights or exercises that require greater effort to keep it growing.
>
> It's the same way with our faith. We put our faith in God to get through a challenge or trial, and later on, another harder trial comes

along. Eventually, we find things that used to bother us or were hard to deal with aren't a problem for us anymore because our faith has grown (https://www.charismamag.com/blogs/straight-talk/20367-learning-to-live-by-faith).

Choosing Faith Over Fear

Joel Osteen uses his knowledge to encourage others to stay focused and continue moving forward. He wants us to know that God has so much more for us if we just keep pressing on. He says:

> Every day, all through the day, you have choices. You can believe that God is in control, believe that He's taking care of you, and believe that good things are in store. Or you can go around worried, expecting the worst, wondering if you will make it.
>
> I often hear fearful people say things like, "I just know my son will fall in with the wrong crowd." They don't realize it, but their words show they're choosing fear over faith.
>
> Fear and faith may seem like opposites, but they have something in common. Both ask us to believe something that we cannot see. Fear says, "Believe the negative." That pain is in your side? That's the same thing your grandmother died from.
>
> That illness is not permanent. It's only temporary.
>
> Faith says, "God is supplying all of your needs."
>
> Fear says, "You've been through too much. You'll never be happy."
>
> Faith says, "Your best days are still out in front of you."

HOW PRAYER CAN WALK YOU THROUGH
THE STORMS IN YOUR LIFE

Here's the key: What you meditate on takes root. If you go around all day thinking about fears, and you play those fears out over and over again in your mind, they will become your reality. That's what Job warned of when he said, "The thing I feared came upon me."

A friend told me recently that everything was going great in his life. He had become engaged. His business was blessed. But instead of enjoying it, instead of thanking God for it, he said, "Joel, I'm afraid it will not last. I'm afraid it's too good to be true."

When you buy into fears, you draw in the negative. You help those fears come to pass. Do not allow them to take root.

Switch over into faith and pray: "Father, You said Your favor will last for a lifetime. You said goodness and mercy will follow me all the days of my life."

Focus on your faith; let God deal with your fear. We have so many opportunities to be fearful in these times. People are concerned about the economy, worried about their health, fearful for their children. But God says to you what He said to me: "Don't use your energy to worry. Use your energy to believe" (Osteen, Joel, "It's Your Time: Activate your Faith, Achieve your Dreams, and Increase in God's Favor." **Running Press**, 2012, pp. 94–96).

10

How to Prepare for the Storms of Life

At the age of ten, I began praying and did not understand what was occurring in my life. As a young adult, I would pray for people when I saw their car pulled over to the side of the road for help. In the early 90's, my pastor asked if I would coordinate the prayer ministry at church in Dallas. I touched him on the forehead and asked if he had lost his holy mind; he immediately responded no. I told him if he felt that I can do this, then I would.

This is what I call God preparing His child for the storms of life because He knew the plan He had for me. God was designing the path He knew I needed to help me because this is how much He loves me. This shows me that God is always in control and working behind the scenes to care for His children.

While attending Southwestern Christian College, I would go to the nightly mission study prepared by the ministerial students. It was so encouraging to hear a message from the Word, and the singing was so uplifting it kept me motivated to return the next night. At this age in my life, I really did not understand the trials of life, but God was preparing me for the rough days in my journey. I had my mind set that I wanted to be fed more spiritually, and it gave me the desire to keep going back for more of the spiritual food. I was already praying

HOW PRAYER CAN WALK YOU THROUGH THE STORMS IN YOUR LIFE

at this point in my life, but I felt so energized when I left the meeting, I would go to my dorm room and just praise God.

As children of God, we know storms will always be a part of our lives, and we can never fully prepare for what will come our way. As God's children, we have assurance that He wants us to be as equipped as possible for this journey. Here are some ways to help prepare for the storms:

1. Stay in church, work in the church, and do not just sit on the pew.
2. Read and study the Word of God daily.
3. Pray and ask God to reveal to you what book He wants you to read and any other suggestions He has for you.
4. Praise God for His goodness.
5. Keep a journal so when you are in a storm, you can look back and see His progress and how you dealt with the previous storm. This will motivate you to keep going and not give up.
6. Please stay connected to a circle of friends who are concerned about living for God.
7. Listen to other people's testimonies; this is a good way for your faith to be increased.
8. Tell God you are available. "Use me however You see fit. Shape me and mold me into who You want me to be."

Charles Stanley reminds us in his book, *Living Close to God*, that we can never be fully prepared for the adversity in our lives. He tells us the following:

Preparing for Adversity

Jesus made it clear: difficulties are to be expected. He told His followers in John 16:33: "These things I have spoken to you, that in Me you may have peace. In the world you have tribulation, but take courage; I have overcome the world."

Adversity is often the common thread that runs through the lives of the men and women mentioned in the Bible. Abraham, Moses, Joseph, Esther, David, Joshua, the prophets, the disciples, Elizabeth, Mary, Paul, and every other major biblical figure wrestled with problems. Adversity is a part of life. The consequences of sin are all around us. Although we can never be fully prepared for all the possibilities, we can take positive steps to fortify our faith to withstand the tough times.

The acceptance of setbacks is, in reality, a type of beginning. It is in acceptance that we truly recognize our need for God. Some things are much too tough for us to handle on our own. Paul could not preach the Gospel to all of Asia Minor by himself. The Sprit of God was his constant companion through trials and tribulations, through laughter and reward, (Stanley, Charles F., *Living Close to God*. Inspirational Press, 1995, p. 207).

11

Seeking Ways to Trust God Through the Storm

I believe if we set our minds to trust God through the storm and totally depend on Him, we will survive the storm with a stronger faith. If we are going to trust God, we must stand on His promises and allow the Holy Spirit to work in our lives. Here are some ways to help trust God on our journey:

1. Begin and end your day with God; let Him know you need His help, and you can't make it without Him.
2. Find a scripture to focus on. I always tell people to put a scripture in their shoe, so when they are walking, they will feel the paper, and it will remind them to pray. You can also thank God for how you are able to trust Him at this point and ask Him for strength to keep trusting Him more. This is a way to have Jesus close to you and feel the peace that only He can give.
3. Quiet time is a must. We need to allow time so we can listen to the Holy Spirit. If our minds are so stressed, we will not be able to hear what God wants to tell us. Tell God, "I am available and waiting for You to speak to me." He may have an answer to something you have been praying

about. Thank God for this quiet time and all the prayers He answered in the past.

4. We must stand on the promises of God. Here are some promises we can hold on to:
    - In Psalm 121 (KJV), God promised protection for His children.
    - Deuteronomy 4:29 (KJV), God promised if we search for Him, we will find Him.
    - First Chronicles 16:34 (KJV), God promised that His love will never fail. He is faithful in every way.
    - Philippians 4:6–7 (KJV), God promised peace when we pray.
    - Matthew 11:28–30 (KJV), God promised rest.
    - Second Corinthians 1:3–4 (KJV), God promised comfort in our trials.
    - Matthew 6:33 and Philippians 4:19 (KJV), God promised to supply our needs.
    - John 4:14 (KJV), God promised eternal life to those who trust Him.

12

Staying Motivated to Pray in the Storm

Staying motivated in the storm can be successful, if we keep our eyes on Jesus. God has given us the tool of prayer as a weapon to fight the spiritual battle. We must be prepared for the battlefield. God wants us to be strong, healthy prayer warriors who can stand the test of times. He is rooting for His children to stay on board and seek His face daily. Staying motivated is seeking help from others; we need relationships and people around us that are striving to live for Christ and are willing to encourage us along this path. Motivation is having the energy or zeal to keep moving, no matter what the storm looks like.

When you pray and ask God for the strength to get through the storm, He will give it to you. He is there to cheer you along the way. He is the best cheerleader you will ever have, and He never gets tired of cheering for you. He wants you to reach the finish line and obtain the prize, which is the reward of being faithful and trusting Him. Storms will continue to come in our lives, so we need to learn how to manage them, keep a positive attitude, and grow in the midst of our pain. Pain allows us to know something is wrong, and we need to make a change in our lives. This is the time to give the pain to God. Pain should be something that desires us to push forward and do what it takes to remove it from our lives. I want to share with you some prayers that I wrote for myself over the years as I faced difficulties in my life. Here are a few of my prayers:

Taking My Eyes Off the Things that Surrounds the Storm

> My Father,
> Help me to take my eyes off all that surrounds my storm.
> Help me to put my focus on You and seek Your face daily.
> I want to learn everything I need to know from the storm so I can share with others my experience.
> Teach me how to walk through the storm correctly, so when I walk out of the storm, I would have gained all I can.
> Help me to be a blessing to someone else as others have blessed me.
> When something catches my attention that takes my focus off You,
> allow the Holy Spirit to tell me to sing... Praise the Lord! Praise the Lord!
> Look at me and watch me my child... Praise the Lord! Praise the Lord!
> Teach me, Lord, to be like You... Praise the Lord! Praise the Lord!
> Shape me, Lord, to look like You... Praise the Lord! Praise the Lord!
> In His precious name, Amen!

Encouragement for Today

> My Father,
> I know You are working on my behalf, and at this time,

HOW PRAYER CAN WALK YOU THROUGH THE STORMS IN YOUR LIFE

I am asking that You will give me some encouragement for today.

I know You work the night shift, and You only want the best for me.

I am still seeking You and waiting on Your answer.

Please help me not to miss my blessing and to clearly hear You when You answer.

Give me the strength to hold on to Your promises and keep the faith.

Thank You for taking care of me.

In the name of Jesus. Amen.

Encouragement While Waiting for the Answer

Father, I stand in need of encouragement, and I am seeking Your face.

I asked that You will give me some encouragement as I wait for Your answers.

I have prayed and prayed, and I am thanking You for the outcome.

Help me to always look to You for all I need.

Give me wisdom to make godly decisions in all I do.

When You answer my prayers, please make it crystal clear,

So I will not have a shadow of doubt that it is what You want me to do.

I know You will give me Your very best. Thank You for being my Father.

In the name of Jesus.

Keep Me on the Path

To my *Daddy*,

I am so grateful that I belong to You.

Please keep me on the path that You have designed for me.

It is my prayer that I keep walking, praying, and asking for Your direction daily.

I am open to whatever You want me to do.

Oh, how I love You and depend on You.

I trust You with my entire life, because it is the life You have given to me.

I do not want to miss any of my blessings.

Help me to hear You clearly and make it crystal clear.

I look forward to walking in the path You have prepared for me.

In the name of Jesus.

Finding a weekly prayer meeting could encourage you throughout your storm. This will allow you to find connections for fellowship and developing new relationships. I like to hear people give testimonies about what they have witnessed God doing in their lives. This is one way we can be motivated to stay on the battlefield. If you speak with someone who just went through what you are experiencing right now, it will put a smile on your face when you hear them talk about our Father and how faithful He is. You can tell yourself, "If God brought her through, He can surely do it for me." This will give you the energy to keep praying and asking God to place people in your life who can encourage you.

I sure like the idea of getting involved in the lives of senior citizens. When we take time to visit them and run errands for them, it takes our mind off of the storm. When we think we are helping the senior citizens, deep down inside, we are helping ourselves. It allows us to get refreshed along the journey and be thankful for the time we can assist someone else.

Since I like to drink coffee, I like to reward myself with a beautiful cup of coffee from Starbucks from time to time. This will motivate me to sit before God with my journal and pen. I can spend time, praying and asking God to reveal new ways for me to seek what I need assistance with. If He reveals for me to purchase a new book, I get so excited about what He wants me to read. I can walk the aisles in the bookstore for hours, looking in the books to see which one I want to purchase. I recall times when I would get a hotel room thirty miles from home for the weekend, just to get away and spend time reading and meditating on the Word. It leaves me refreshed and wanting to continue walking throughout the storm because I have confidence that I can do it with God's help. I know I can rely on Him and stand boldly on His promises. Once I claim the promise I need, I continue to pray and allow God to work things out for me.

You can start a prayer meeting at your church and place all the answered prayers on the bulletin board. This will surely encourage you, once people begin to trust God and bring their requests to Him. Before you know it, the bulletin board will be full of people's names that have answers to their prayers. The people who are still waiting for God to answer their prayers will also be encouraged.

The Benefits of Journaling

When you take the time to sit and write your thoughts out, it helps you to shed some of the everyday stress. Our lives are so busy; we need to slow down and enjoy a slower pace. When we take time to think, things become a little clearer to us, and we appear to be able to manage our time better. I feel like I can release my cares during my journaling time and be refreshed.

When I write about my thoughts, somehow, it takes the weight off my shoulder. God may be trying to tell me something during this time. I like to share with God how my day went and tell Him what I am thankful for. I lay my requests before Him and let Him know I am available and waiting for Him to speak to me.

Once you have cleared your mind and cast your cares, you can rest in the Lord with peace. It feels good to be able to get a good night's sleep, so you can start your journey the next day refreshed.

Sometimes, I pick up a journal from years ago and read about when I walked through a certain trial. I find myself saying, "I did that." What, or wow. I can see my progress and how I handled things at that time in my life. Some of the journaling leaves me saying, "Thank you, Lord, for taking care of me during that time." Of course, I also have some journaling where I just want to hide the journal altogether, but thank God for the good and the bad because this is growth in my life. I just like reading my journals to see how I have grown in my faith over the years. Sometimes, if I am in a storm, I will look back in my journal to see how I handled this situation before and how I can approach it now. It is encouraging to see yourself handling difficult things in a godly way.

Having a Positive Mindset for Christ

We hear people say keep a positive outlook on things and you will go far in life. I truly believe thinking positive helps you get through the tough times in life. It keeps your mind focused on good thoughts for the future. You can be experiencing a difficulty, but if you set your mind, you can look for the good that will come out of this day.

In the article by Remez Sasson, he shares five reasons why you should think positively. He shares the following:

1. Happiness

    A positive attitude awakens happiness. You don't have to be rich or achieve goals to be happy. It is a matter of attitude. When you adopt a positive frame of mind, you become happy. Happiness does not depend on external causes. It comes from inside you.

2. Motivation

    Motivation is a positive quality and a wonderful trait to have. It pushes you forward, encourages you, and helps you overcome obstacles.

3. Self-Esteem

Choose to look at yourself in a positive light. See what is positive and good in you.

4. Better Health

The mind has a strong effect on the body and on health. When you think positively, your immune system is healthier, and your body recuperates faster.

5. Improved relations

Another reason why you should adopt a positive way of thinking is the effect it has on relations with people. People tend to gravitate towards positive people and keep their distance from negative people. Positive people bring joy, happiness, and uplifting energy, and are fun to be around (https://www.successconsciousness.com).

Renovating Your Mind

Our soul has stored memories, experiences, events, failures, and disappointments—all types of pain from the past. This is a large warehouse of things stored, and we must clean out the house. We have all types of baggage in our souls, and our souls need to be restored.

When we think about the years of pain we have carried around year after year and never given it to God, it begins to weigh on our shoulders. God does not want us living like this.

He wants us to clean out our storage so this weight will not wear us down.

Paul speaks of renewing your mind in Romans 12:2; to renovate your mind means to remake it. Romans 12:2 states, "And be not conformed to this world: but be ye transformed by the renewing of your mind, that ye may prove what is that good, and acceptable, and perfect will of God." The mind is changed by prayer and reading the Word of God. When we reflect on God, we can see a change in our life.

> Our thoughts become words.
> Our words become actions.
> Our actions become a habit.
> Our habit becomes our character.
> Our character becomes our destiny.
> (Unknown author)

I like these words from the unknown author. When I think of my thoughts, I want them to be pleasing to God and knowing that my words become my actions. My actions will describe me, and I have to ensure my actions are pleasing to God because they become a habit. It only takes twenty-one days to form a habit and much longer to break one. My habit will become my character. I believe in doing the right thing, no matter where I am. My character becomes my destiny. I want to enjoy working in the place God has designed for me to work.

It all goes back to the mind. When we set our mind and stay focused on God's benefits, we can walk through the storms with peace. Our destiny is what we want to be striving for in this life. When God created us, He knew exactly what He put us here on Earth to do. It is my goal to reach my destiny; I want to enjoy this part of my life. When we operate in the will of God, He will keep us on the path to our destiny.

Once we have cleaned the baggage from our lives, we must continue to move forward. We have new opportunities, new people to see, and new places to go. God is wanting to do great things in our lives. We have to be willing to take the risk. We have nothing to lose and everything to gain. God is on the battlefield with us and cheering us along the way.

Once the renovating is over, we must keep working to ensure the baggage doesn't creep back into storage. It is easy for the storage room to become full, but it is harder to clean it out. We must depend on God to help us in this area. We need to feed our thoughts with words that are encouraging. When the disappointments come, we must understand everything we can about it so we can move forward and not dwell on it. We are not perfect, so from time to time, we will have failures in our lives. We have to take the failures and look for something good in the midst of it. This could be an opportunity for you to turn it into a blessing.

God is always at work in our lives. We need to ask Him where He is working so we can join in with Him. Ask God to show you what He is up to in your life, then wait patiently as He reveals it to you. Take the time to journal your answers so you can be amazed at how He shares His answers with you.

Questions You Can Ask God When You Are in a Storm

Here are some questions to ask God in prayer and remember to always thank Him every day. Please make sure your prayers are in line with His will for your life.

1. Ask God for wisdom.
2. Lord, how can I understand the storm from Your perspective?
3. Ask for guidance every day.
4. Ask the Lord to help you quiet your mind so you can listen to Him and make godly decisions.
5. Ask the Lord to put people in your life who will encourage you.
6. Ask God for encouragement.
7. Please reveal to me if there is any sin in my life that I am unaware of.
8. Ask God for peace and anything else you need.
9. Ask God to help you wait on His answer and not to take things in your own hands.
10. Ask God to help you trust Him throughout the process.
11. How can I grow in maturity with this storm?

12. Please show me how to walk through this storm and bring you glory.
13. Lord, please show me if I have overlooked anything I need to know.
14. Ask God for strength and endurance.

From time to time, we all face some type of storm in various ways. I want us to understand the difference between a storm and a consequence. We must keep in mind, as earlier stated, a storm is a trial, tragedy, or misfortune. A consequence is defined as a result or effect, typically one that is unwelcome or unpleasant (englishoxford-livingdictionaries.com). When we try to take things into our own hands and mess them up, there are consequences that come with this type of behavior.

Here are some examples of storms

1. Mary lost her job due to a decrease in residents applying for service.
2. John is unable to work due to a car accident and applying for disability benefits.
3. Financial hardship.
4. A difficulty on your job.
5. A conflict with family members/friends.
6. Health concerns.
7. Church conflict.
8. Death of a family member.
9. Losing your home or business.
10. Tax problems.
11. Child behavior problems.
12. Divorce.
13. Cheating spouse.
14. Abusive relationships.

The Master's Peace

When we are in the midst of a storm, we must cry out to God and let Him know we need direction and peace as we trust Him. I even pray for step-by-step direction because I do not want to miss anything. I recall when I first started to pray for faith, I would tell God to just give me a little clue that He was working. I told Him I needed some encouragement, and yes, He gave me the encouragement I needed. I kept a list of prayers with the dates that God answered my prayers. I could not wait to get a cup of coffee and my journal and just be amazed at how God took care of me. In the midst of my pain, I continued to converse with God and let Him know my needs and that I needed peace.

Life is a journey, and when we are in the storms, we need to rest and have the peace that only God can give. I find myself praying day after day for peace and the zeal to keep on going. God showed up and showed out in my life. When I ask, He gives; when I seek, I find Him waiting for me. I must say this is a beautiful experience when we use prayer to help us.

I love to hear people say that when God guides you, He always provides. This is the same thing as we walk through the stormy times; He gives us the tools we need to survive the storms.

We must be willing to use them.

I remember times when I have tossed and turned throughout the night because I did not have God's peace. It is very difficult to get a good night's sleep when you are restless and concerned about things we have no control over any way. God tells us to cast our cares upon Him. I would get out of bed, get my Bible, turn to the book of Psalms, and start reading and meditating on the Word. When I said my prayer and went back to bed, I could sleep.

I recall a sister in church once told me that the majority of my storms will come from my jobs. I kept those words close to my heart. I truly believe this is one of the reasons I kept praying and staying close to God, because when an older woman tells me something, I am eager to listen. I must say, today, a majority of my storms have been on my jobs. I have shed many tears due to the storms on my jobs. I will be the first to tell you how happy I am to have had the opportunity to experience the storms in my life from my jobs. Those storms are the reason for who I am today—a child of God who totally depends on Him and prays to Him about everything. I have learned a lot from the storms, but life is always a learning process.

When I began to experience storms on my jobs in my younger years, I told God there was no reason I should have to go through all this pain. I had no idea what storms were and how to deal with them or even working in the type of environments I worked in. We all know dealing with people can be a challenge at times, but we must continue to let our light shine. I would take my lunch breaks and drive to the lake and sit in the car and pray during my lunch hour. I would thank God for helping me through the first four hours of the work day and request His assistance with the remaining four hours. I remember I had purchased a book while attending Lubbock Christian University called *Christians in Pain* by B. W. Woods. I read the "Christian Perspective" chapter which reads, "And we know that to them that love God, all things work together for good, even to them that are called according to his purpose" (Romans 8:28). I knew I needed to grow spiritually, but not this way.

B. W. Woods stated in another chapter that life is a school, and suffering is one of the instructors. For this reason, Christians are not exempt. The heavenly Father cares too much about us to let us go on in ignorance. He desires our maturity, and maturity does not come easily. Some lessons are not learned apart from suffering (Woods, B. W., *Christians in Pain*. Baker Book House. 1982, p. 23).

When I began to understand a little about storms and how to live for God, I started a mini library with books that helped me along my path. I would seek ways to keep myself encouraged; I would ask God to help me speak when I need to speak and be silent when I need to be silent. I would wear a rubber band on my wrist; if I felt stressed, or someone said something unpleasant, and I wanted to pray before I responded to them, I would pull the rubber band to remind myself to pray first.

I must say, no matter how many storms I face on my jobs, God will be right there with me as I walk this journey. We learn so much about people as we continue to spend time with them at work. They know you are a child of God, and some of them will test you to see how you respond. They will wait to see if you change and become a part of their circle. I believe they truly admire you for being who you are and, sometimes, may even want to find out more about God and how He works in your life. This is why it is so important, as Christians, that we be an example of Christ and do the right thing even if no one is looking. People are watching us and waiting to see how we treat them. I work long hours sometimes, but as I am up and down those halls, I am praying as I am working. As a Christian, we must show our love; this is what our coworkers need to see from us. When someone mistreats you, and you can still be kind and loving to them, it shows them the love of Christ. Life is not easy, but it is so much better having a Father who can manage our actions.

When we are faced with a storm on our job, we must use it to our advantage, just like any other storm. Sometimes, we don't understand why people act the way they do. Some people do what they see their friends or co-workers do to fit in. If you will take the time to talk with them, they will ask you questions about your spiritual journey. For example, they may ask you where you attend church and the time for the service. I truly believe this conversation about God and church can lead to another one, and eventually, the person will come to church. This person shared with me about other people having problems and how they need to go to church.

Sometimes, people just need someone to listen to how they feel so they know that someone cares. A concern came up in this person's life, so she went home early. After I ate dinner, I texted this young lady to see if she was okay. She texted me back to say that she was okay, and it was good to know that someone cared about her. So I texted back to say, "Of course, people care about you." I used this as an example of what God wants us to do in the life of other people. I am sure someone took out time to do this for us in the past. This not only makes the person feel better but feel valued as well. This was a great opportunity for me to pray for this person. My actions showed this person how Christ wants us to live.

We must keep in mind our character is who we really are, not who we say we are. I have to do the right thing in the life of anyone who crosses my path. I do not want to live one way at work and another way at home. I want to be the light in my workplace because Christ lives in me. I do not mind being the only person standing up for what is right because I know it is the right thing to do. I will be able to go home and sleep in peace.

We had a meeting at work, and each person was given a piece of paper to write our name on it. Once we wrote our name, we were asked to write one word to describe the person whose name was on the paper when it came to us. Once we completed the task, the last person with your paper will read what the coworkers said about you. This is how my coworkers described me:

1. Very kind
2. Goes above and beyond for residents
3. So kind and considerate
4. Honest and caring
5. Nice and funny
6. Honest
7. You can tell her anything.
8. Young
9. Kind and considerate

HOW PRAYER CAN WALK YOU THROUGH THE STORMS IN YOUR LIFE

10. Best person we met in a long time.
11. Most professional, caring, and humble

When my name was called, and the person read my paper, it put a smile on my face.

It reminded me of how God wants His children to represent Him. The words that stand out the most to me are kind, honest, and caring. I can look at these words and know that from the pain I have experienced in my life, God uses it to make me a better person. The pain is what continues to encourage me to hold on to His hands, not just in the difficult times but at all times.

When I go through future storms on my job, I can pull out this list of ways my coworkers have described me and stay encouraged. It is nice to work with a group of people who know you are honest and they can depend on you to do the right thing.

We all have challenging jobs that take a lot of our time and energy. It appears that we are at work longer than at home sometimes. We must realize, no matter what type of environment we are placed in, God still expects us to be an example. I want the people that I work with to know that I belong to Christ, and He rules and regulates in my life.

Dealing with difficult people on the job is just part of the training process. We must learn how to get along with all people, whether they are nice or unpleasant. When I pray, I ask God to show me how to deal with the personalities I am faced with. Difficult people have good days and bad days just like we do. I think when we try to find a way to help make their day a little better, this does seem to help the situation. We don't realize what the difficult person is going through on any given day. They may have received a phone call about a family member not doing well or is in the hospital, and they are trying to deal with that. We all deal with our problems in a different way.

I asked God to work on me so I can have what it takes to function in this type of environment. I walk around some days, truly saying I love my job, and the reason is because I can see the joy in it. I am helping people and empowering them. I don't want to focus my time and energy on problems but allowing the Holy Spirit to show me how to walk in the midst of difficulties and shine. God is helping me to face anything I need to face on my job, and I trust Him that I will come out victorious.

I really observe the way cashiers are treated by customers. One day, I was in line at the store; the line was long, but the cashier was very friendly. When I got closer to the register, the young lady in front of me had a bad attitude and said some unkind words to the cashier. The cashier continued to treat the customer with respect; she even told her, "Thank you for coming in." This cashier did not let the customer's unkind words make her feel bad. She kept doing her job with a smile. When it came my turn to be waited on, I told her thank you for handling that situation in a positive way. I apologized to her for the customer's behavior. She said, "Oh, it is okay, I am fine." I am sure when the customer got to her car and thought about the way she treated this cashier, she felt bad.

I've read that storms are an opportunity for a testimony. I love to hear testimonies of how people have trusted God in the midst of their storms without complaining. I also realized I can help someone else who may be experiencing problems on their job.

Not long ago, I received a call from a friend who needed to talk, and of course, it was about a problem on her job. God is an amazing God. He knows exactly what we need when we need it. He knows what storms we need in 2019 so we will be prepared for 2020. We need to tap into the tools God has for us to live a life depending on Him. This will help us to be able to sleep good at night and not be anxious for anything. I focus on Isaiah 55:17 NIV which reads, "No weapon forged against you will prevail, and you will refute every tongue that accuses you." This verse gives me a lot of peace. I can trust God that He will take care of everything in my life. He promises protection for His children. Here are a few scriptures to keep in mind that can give you peace as you travel throughout your journey.

1. Psalms 91:9–10 reads, "If you make the Most High your dwelling—even the Lord, who is my refuge—then no harm will befall you, no disaster will come near your tent" (NIV).

2. Proverbs 3:24 reads, "When you lie down, you will not be afraid; when you lie down, your sleep will be sweet" (NIV).
3. Psalms 121:7–8 reads, "The Lord will keep you from all harm—He will watch over your life; The Lord will watch over your coming and going, both now and forevermore" (NIV).
4. Deuteronomy 31: 6 reads, "Be strong and courageous. Do not be afraid or terrified because of them, for the Lord your God goes with you; He will never leave you nor forsake you" (NIV).

In this article by Francis Dixon, she shares with us that it is possible to experience a deep-down calm and inward peace from God. She tells us the following:

The Promise of Peace in the Midst of the Storm

1. *Notice what this blessing is that is offered to us*

It is described as "perfect peace." But can we define that? Yes, it is a condition of freedom from disturbance; it is perfect harmony reigning within us. The Hebrew word "shalom" has in it the idea of soundness of health, so that to be filled with perfect peace is to be spiritually healthy and free from discord within our souls. There can be no room for jealousy, envy, uncontrolled temper, selfishness, pride, intolerance, harsh criticism, fear, or anxiety in the soul that is filled with peace; all these things are disturbing factors in our hearts and discordant notes. The peace which God offers, and which by His grace we may experience, is very practical. It is a great calm which He commands (Mark 4:39). God calls His peace "perfect peace." In what sense is it perfect?

- *It is perfect in its quality.* This is to say, it is perfect in the kind of peace it gives. There is an imperfect peace of ignorance when we imagine that all is going well, whereas in fact, all is not well (Jeremiah 6:14). There is the imperfect peace of stagnation. The pool of water may be calm and peaceful, but underneath, it is foul and green with slime. Many men and women know only a peace like that, and one day, the shock of God's judgment will stir up their pool, and they will find that they have no real peace at all (Isaiah 57:14). Then there is the imperfect peace of dependence, which is peace dependent upon some thing or some person in this world. The "thing" may fail, the person may die—and where then is their peace? In contrast, God's peace is perfect.
- *It is perfect in its quantity.* That is to say, the supply of it is sufficient and it exactly meets our need. The marginal rendering of "perfect peace" is "perfect peace"—that is double peace. Notice the significance of this in Philippians 4:7 where we read that this double peace is the peace of heart and of mind; and that is the kind of peace we need, a peace that garrisons our mind and calms our heart. It is also double peace in the sense that it is peace with God (Romans 5:1), and the peace of God (Philippians 4:7), and we can never know the peace of God until we know peace with God.

- *It is perfect in its constancy.* It is permanent and not intermittent. The promise says, "You will keep…"—compare Psalm 121:4.

2. *How does the perfect peace come to us?*

    - *By Christ Jesus.* In Philippians 4:7, we read that the Lord Jesus Christ is the source from whom God's peace flows into our souls. It is the possession of the Christian alone; there is no peace for anyone who does not possess Christ and who is not resting on the finished work of Christ for salvation, thereby "making peace through His blood shed on the cross." Read Colossians 1:19–20.
    - *By the Holy Spirit.* The Lord Jesus Christ procured peace on the Cross of Calvary and it is offered to us by Him as the source; but it is conveyed to our hearts and minds by the Holy Spirit (Galatians 5:22). As the Holy Spirit fills and floods our lives, so He produces this fruit within us.
    - *By His Word.* Have you ever noticed the great promise made in Psalm 119:165? A better rendering of "stumble" is "disturb." How often things and people disturb us! But here is a promise of perfect peace to those who love, meditate in, and obey the Word of God.
    - *By our obedience.* Please look up Leviticus 26:3–6 and notice the most important word here is the word "if."

God guarantees us that if we will do our part, He will surely do His part.
- *By plenty of prayer and praise.* Notice the promise of Philippians 4:7 is preceded by the conditions mentioned in verse 6.

3. *Two conditions must be met if we would experience perfect peace*

Who will God keep in perfect peace? The one "whose mind is steadfast" and the one who "trusts." Both of these expressions denote faith, but one is a head word, and the other one is a heart word. What is the difference? With the head, we believe that God is the author and giver of peace and that He is able and willing to give it; and with the heart, we trust Him to do it, so receive it by faith.

Isaiah 26:3 begins with God and ends with God; it begins with "you" and ends with "you," and the trusting soul goes in between. Perfect peace is the Lord Himself within us—not an experience, a doctrine, an "it," a code of belief—but the Lord Himself (https://www.wordsoflife.co.uk/bible-studies/study-8-the-promise-of-peace-in-the-midst-of-storm)!

In the book *How to let God Solve Your Problems*, Charles Stanley encourages us to wait on God and not try to take things in our own hands. This will help us remain in peace. He writes the following:

Living with a Sense of Perfect Peace

David learned to wait before the Lord, and we need to do the same. God's timing is perfect. He knows when to tell you to move forward.

HOW PRAYER CAN WALK YOU THROUGH THE STORMS IN YOUR LIFE

Until He does, you can rest knowing that the Prince of Peace is at work in your life. When trouble comes, we think, *I've got to do something.* An opportunity presents itself, and we jump at it. People sink deeper into debt because they refuse to be still and listen for God's guidance. They jump ahead of the Lord and then wonder why their lives are so troubled. Before they know it, they have added layer upon layer of problems that they cannot control. This can be true of someone who has lost a spouse or job. The death of a loved one is devastating. Being laid off from a job we like can strike hard against our self-esteem.

After the sudden death of his wife, a middle-aged man announced to his friends that he could not be alone. He needed a wife. Therefore, he remarried and quickly risked bypassing God's best to meet a need in his life. He did not even know if what he was doing was right. He just knew that he had a need and could not wait any longer. Loneliness is not something only single people face. It is something that comes from not being at peace in God's presence and not being satisfied with what He has provided. A person can be lonely even in a room full of people. Never allow loneliness to drive you to do something that you will regret later. God has your need well within His sight, and He will meet it according to His timetable (Stanley, Charles F., *How to Let God Solve Your Problems.* 2008, pp 98–99).

In the article "Love Worth Finding: Finding Peace in the Midst of Your Storm," Adrian Rogers encourages us, as we face tough times, to keep our mind focused on the five truths that will help us keep the peace. The five truths are as follows:

Providence. His purpose brought me here.

Entreaty. His prayers protect me here.
Assurance. His presence comes to me here.
Comfort. His power enables me here.
Expectation. His promise assures me here (http://www/lwf.org/ Copyright 2018).

The article by CBN.com speaks on the subject of peace, it states the following:

Keys to Powerful Living: Peace

If you are having trouble finding peace in your life, you must first understand the source of the conflict that is troubling you. This war within has little to do with your surroundings and has everything to do with your soul.

The Bible says that, apart from Christ, we are "far from God." We are actually His enemies (Colossians 1:21).

Since mankind was originally created for fellowship with God (Genesis 3:8; Genesis 5:1), this separation from Him robs us of peace. Our own sinful actions leave us "without hope and without God" (Ephesians 2:12).

(CBN.com, 2019, The Christian Broadcasting Network, Inc.)

14

The Right Plan from God

Jentezen Franklin shares with us that we are on an assignment from God, and it can't be messed up by our circumstance. He writes the following:

> Know the Source
>
> Jeremiah 29:11 says, "For I know the thoughts that I think toward you, says the Lord, thoughts of peace and not of evil, to give you a future and a hope." God made you for a purpose. When you don't know why something is made, you can easily abuse it. Don't ask the creation what its purpose is; ask its Creator.
>
> Some of you may be thinking, *You don't know where I came from, the things I've done. You don't know my parents. I came from an illegitimate background.* That doesn't matter to God. Here's what you need to understand: "Before I formed you in the womb, I knew you; before you were born, I sanctified you; I ordained you" (Jeremiah 1:5). You don't come from a background. You don't come from your parents. You may have

come through them, but you didn't come from them. You come from God.

Ephesians 2:10 reminds us, "For we are His workmanship, created in Christ Jesus for good works, which God prepared beforehand that we should walk in them." When you were created, God encoded you for an assignment, and He gave you the power to get it done. The enemy's job is to pull us out of that divine assignment, out of the will of God.

The good news is that God has the "inside information" on our lives. First John 2:20 says, "But you have an anointing from the Holy One, and you know all things." Do you have questions in your mind? Do you wonder whom you should marry? Do you wonder what you should do with your life? Do you wonder if you should make that investment? "You have an anointing from the Holy One, and you know all things."

This means that you can know things you were never educated for. You can tap into a resource, an information source called the Holy Spirit, and you can know things that are beyond your natural education or ability to know. The Holy Spirit is smarter than any human being on Earth, and through Him, you can "know all things" (Franklin, Jentezen, *Right People, Right Place, Right Plan: Discerning the Voice of God*. Whitaker House, 2017, pp 112–113).

Beautiful Diamond

This is where God takes all the pain, mistakes, and circumstances in our lives and turns it into something beautiful for His glory. I must say, after all the pain and suffering that has taken place in my life, I will be happy to accept the diamond. A diamond coming from God is a beautiful thing, and I will be smiling from ear to ear and praising Him at the same time. I can only thank God for where the pain has brought me from in my life to where I am with Him today. I can only give Him the glory because my life is about living for Him.

At this point in my life, I thank God for the opportunities that my trials have brought me. I look back in my journal from time to time to be reminded of how God worked things out in my past. I know some storms I created for myself, I can never take them back, but I sure have learned from them. God used my storms to bring about a change in my life for various reasons, and I say thank You, God, for being a good *Daddy*. He corrects His children because He only wants what's best for them. In Hebrews 12:4–12 (NIV), the Bible states the following:

> In your struggle against sin, you have not yet resisted to the point of shedding your blood.
> And have you completely forgotten this word of encouragement that addresses you as a father addresses his son? It says, "My son, do not make light of the Lord's discipline, and do not lose heart when He rebukes you,
> "because the Lord disciplines the one He loves, and He chastens everyone He accepts as His son."
> Endure hardship as discipline; God is treating you as His children. For what children are not disciplined by their father?
> If you are not disciplined—and everyone undergoes discipline—then you are not legitimate, not true sons and daughters at all.
> Moreover, we have all had human fathers who disciplined us, and we respected them for it. How much more should we submit to the Father of spirits, and live!

> They disciplined us for a little while as they thought best; but God disciplines us for our good in order that we may share in his holiness.
>
> No discipline seems pleasant at the time, but painful. Later on, however, it produces a harvest of righteousness and peace for those who have been trained by it.
>
> Therefore, strengthen your feeble arms and weak knees.

God is working on me so I can be all that He has created me to be. I do not want to leave this Earth without receiving all He has for me. I want to reach my purpose in life—what God predestined me to be. I must also say I want a long life to enjoy this experience. This is one reason why I love Jeremiah 29:11(NIV) which reads, "'For I know the plans I have for you,' declares the LORD, 'plans to prosper you and not harm you, plans to give you hope and a future.'" I know it will be good because my *Father* is a good God, and He loves His child.

Sometimes, we hear people talking about a pastor that really has a heart to preach the Word. Well, that heart probably has experienced all kinds of pain and allowed God to do a work in Him. This person spends time in the Word, preparing, so when he stands in front of the pulpit and preaches, you can see God in his life. This is a man after God's heart. Some people have a gift to preach that came from God; they spend time preparing so they can exercise this gift.

When I teach in the prisons, I spend time preparing myself, because when I stand in front of the class, I want to give them an encouraging word from the Lord. I want them to see Christ in me because I am a representative of God. He sends me to do His work, and I take it very serious.

15

God Really Does Have a Purpose Behind Your Problems!

In this article by Dr. Richard J. Krejcir, he tells us we need to see the joy and opportunities through times of problems. He writes:

> God is our refuge and strength!
>
> If we are going through tough times, we need to know why and what we should do when we are in them. If not, we become confused, frustrated, and disillusioned. Yet in the Psalms, we see David go through so much and still trust and obey more than most of us could ever do. And he does this without the New Testament at his disposal, or the scores of resources and places to seek help that we have. Yet David does ask God the hard questions, but he did not stop there. David also knew God intimately and trusted Him wholeheartedly even in times of severe trials, and even

going through them again and again. Just read through the Psalms and see David's passion and conviction to God's call.

We must first adjust the way we perceive life. Even as Christians, sometimes, we have faulty views and expectations we pick up by listening to bad teaching and bad advice, and then there is the influence of our culture. First of all, bad things do happen! And they happen to good people (in the way we see good, in God's eyes, of course, all have sinned and there is no good except what Christ brings us). We will go through trials, troubles, and tribulations. So what we have to do is figure out what we should do when it happens. What lesson can we learn from it so we can grow and not become bitter? We simply need to stand on His promise. Read Psalm 46:1.

God does not look upon trouble as we do. Where we see stress, He sees opportunities.

Where we see crisis, He sees growth and betterment. God's purpose in times of crisis and trouble is to teach His children precious lessons. They are intended to educate and build us up. And when we learn from them and ride out these storms of life, we will see the great purpose fulfilled. His glorious recompense will come to us throughout eternity. We need to see the joy and opportunities through times of problems. Because we will learn that there is a sweet and wonderful joy filled by seizing the crisis and growing from it. To become the person that we are capable of being for our benefit and His glory.

So when God tests you, or bad stuff happens, we need to see it as a time for you to learn and to trust Him. It's by these trials that He's changing what is wrong with you while putting

His promises in your heart and feet. And when it is over, we can look back and see that our trials have been necessary. We are better, He is glorified!

To be a content Christian and happy with life, we need to see life as a series of problem-solving and learning opportunities. Because the problems we face will either overwhelm and overpower us or grow and develop us. Thus, the path of joy is determined by how we respond to them. Unfortunately, most people, including Christians, will fail to see God's hand in their life, choosing instead to focus on their problem and allowing it to take over their lives: Like a terrorist holding them at gunpoint and refusing to allow the help to rescue them.

God wants to use our problems for good, to make us better and stronger for our personal development, and in turn, for us to be able to help others in their lives. So the unhappy, confused, and disillusioned Christian will react irrationally with their problems rather than taking the time through spiritual discipline to see the advantage they bring them. So what can we do to refocus ourselves onto the right path?

During my times of adversity, I have learned five ways God will use the problems in your life:

1. *God uses problems to examine you.*

People can be like canned food without the label; if you want to know what's inside, just open them up. Does God need to open you up? When has God tested your faith with a problem? How did you respond? What did you learn? What do you think going through problems will reveal about you? Is your will and desire ruling over you, or is Christ the true Lord of your life?

2. *God uses problems to lead you in the right direction.*

Sometimes God needs to slap us in the face to wake us up. Without such wakeup calls, we will blindly fall onto the wrong path that leads to greater disappointment and ruin. We will not see it coming because our will is in the way of His. But know this, God is there leading and protecting us, even when we do not see Him. And be warned, if your will is in the way of His, He will light a fire under you to get you moving. If He didn't, it would show He does not love you. Just as a parent will discipline their child out of love, problems will point us in a right direction if we surrender our will over to His. His love is there to motivate us and change us. This puts us on the best path for our life and gives us a plan much better than we could ever come up with. Is God trying to get your attention?

3. *God uses problems to discipline you.*

Sometimes, the only way to learn the lessons in life and to make us better is by suffering and failure. It is like a child being told by its parents not to touch a hot stove. And we all have touched that hot stove. Thus, we learned by being burned. Now, know this, God is not up there getting His jollies by infecting us, not at all. He loves us so much. He will resort to what He has to do to bring us up closer to Him. Remember He sacrificed His own Son, and the extreme pain Jesus went through for us. Pain is a part of life, so it is best we accept and learn from it so we do not have to keep getting burned. Most people only learn the value of something such as health, money, or relationships by losing them.

4. *God uses problems to shield you from greater harm.*

Problems can be a blessing in disguise, because they can prevent us from being harmed by something more severe. Such as a car breaking down just before it reaches the railroad tracks as a train is zooming by. Car breakdowns are stressful and costly, but the train is even more so. Just as the story of Joseph, he suffered needlessly from our perspective, but God protected him and turned it into incredible good.

5. *God uses problems to refine and improve you.*

Problems are the main ingredients for us to build character. The key to these building materials is that they need to be used in the right way to be able to fit and function correctly. And that right way is how we respond and learn. God is far more interested in our character than our comfort. In the grand scheme of things, the meaning of life, the reason we live the life we are given, is our relationship with God, and then others around us. So the most important thing we have in those relationships is our character, the only two things we will take into eternity is relationships and character (http://www.discipleshiptools.org/apps/articles/default.asp?articleid=37254).

In this article, by R David Jones, he speaks on the same subject. He states the following:

The Benefits of Trials

Times of hardship are times of learning. In Hebrews 12, we see that one method God uses in the life of the believer is chastening, which literally means "child training." God says there is a reason for them, and it is a good reason. "And we know that all things work together for good to them that love God, to them who are called according to his purpose" (Romans 8:28).

We know that God is working something out in our lives. This does not necessarily mean that we are always able to understand what purpose God has in it. This is the positive test of genuine faith. Someone has expressed it like this: "The acid of grief tests the coin of belief."

God must send us trouble so that we learn patience, which will also produce hope and love in the lives of men and women. Sometimes, when problems come, we become desperate and use frantic means to cut the storm short. We should never become despondent or discouraged when passing through trials. Some problems in life are never removed. We must learn to accept them and to prove that His grace is sufficient. Paul, for an example, asked the Lord three times to remove a physical infirmity. The Lord did not remove it but gave Paul the grace to bear it (2 Corinthians 12:8–10).

When trials come upon us, it is our faith which will carry us through, and God will provide the wisdom if we believe Him. He will be glad to help us out and does not reproach us for depending on Him. If we feel we are not capable of living in the present difficult times, we have a heavenly Father who can supply the wisdom that we need (http://www.bible-facts.info/commentaries/nt/james/james1v3_12.htm).

This article further explains adversity. The writer states the following:

What Are God's Purposes for Allowing Adversity in My Life?

Understanding Adversity

The Apostle Paul expressed a similar perspective on adversity: "We glory in tribulations also: knowing that tribulation worketh patience; and patience, experience; and experience, hope: and hope maketh not ashamed; because the love of God is shed abroad in our hearts by the Holy Ghost which is given unto us. For when we were yet without strength, in due time Christ died for the ungodly" (Romans 5:3–6). Here are some of God purposes for the adversity in our lives.
1. Adversity gets our attention.
2. Adversity reminds us of our weaknesses.
3. Adversity motivates us to fear the Lord.
4. Adversity strengthens our hatred for sin.
5. Adversity is a call for self-examination.
6. Adversity exposes pride.
7. Adversity is God's method of purifying our faith.
8. Adversity tests our friendships (https://ibip.org)

In the article by Tony Evans, he shares with us some information on why God allows trials in our life. He shares the following:

When God Allows Your Trial

Have you ever received a letter that wasn't addressed to you personally? Instead, it was simply labeled, *Occupant.* You get that piece of mail because you're the occupant of your home. Trials are a lot like that. Just by virtue of being an occupant of this fallen world, we will face trials.

Of course, no one likes a trial. No one wakes up in the morning, stretches, and says, "Ah, what a beautiful day for a trial! I think I'd like to have a trial today!" Only an unusual person would do something like that. Yet regardless of how much we want to avoid trials in our lives, they are inevitable.

Trials are adverse circumstances that God allows in our lives to identify where we are spiritually and to prepare us for where He wants us to go. We cannot escape trials. Either you are in a trial now, you've just come out of a trial, or you're getting ready to go into a trial.

But even though we all have to experience them, you can take comfort in knowing that trials must first pass through God's hands before reaching us. Nothing comes our way without first having received His divine approval. And if a trial is to receive His divine approval, He must have a divine reason to approve it. We need to trust that God has our best interests in mind when He allows us to experience trials (https://tonyevans.org/when-God-allows-your-trial).

In the article "The Battle Isn't Ours to Fight," Creflo Dollar shares with us:

When we see trouble on the horizon, He'll protect us. If we're already in it, He'll deliver us. When we're in the midst of something, we must focus on how we'll get out of the dilemma. "He shall call upon Me, and I will answer him: I will be with him in trouble; I will deliver him and honor him." (Psalm 91:15). God makes a way when it seems there is no way.

God's pledge to rescue us when we call to Him for help brings real results. Many of us can remember tough situations that made us feel helpless and alone, and the only thing we could think of to do was pray. Regardless of what anyone may tell us, prayerfully asking Him for protection isn't a sign of weakness, but of strength. "The angel of the Lord encamped round about them that fear Him and delivered them. Many are the afflictions of the righteous: but the Lord delivered him out of them all" (Psalm 34:7, 19).

God is unshakeable and immovable, and He's stronger than any fortress we could ever build for ourselves. "For who is God, except the Lord? And who is a rock, except our God?" (Psalm 18:31 NKJV). His mercy and love is infinite, and He'll never let us down when we depend on Him for our security. The debilitating, paralyzing fear that roams the world has no power over us when we make God our protector (https://creflodollarministries.org/Bible-Study/Articles/The-Battles-Isn't-Ours-to-Fight).

In the book, by Joel Osteen, *Your Best Life Now: 7 Steps to Living at Your Full Potential*, he shares with us that it is in the tough times of life that we find out what we're made of. He states the following:

The Purpose of Trials

The pressure exposes things that we need to deal with—things such as wrong attitudes, wrong motives, areas where we're compromising. As odd as this may seem, the trials can be beneficial.

The trial is intended to test your quality, to test your character, to test your faith. In other words, "Don't think it's a big deal when you go through these tough times." All through life, you will face various tests, and even though you may not enjoy them, God will use those trials to refine you, to cleanse, and purify you. He's trying to shape you into the person He wants you to be. If you will learn to cooperate with God and be quick to change and correct the areas that He brings to light, then you'll pass that test, and you will be promoted to a new level (Osteen, Joel, *Your Best Life Now: 7 Steps to Living at Your Full Potential*. Pp. 205–206).

In the book *How to Let God Solve Your Problems*, Charles Stanley speaks on the subject of pressure. He indicates the following:

How to Find Clear Guidance

When it comes to making right decisions, I believe this is the greatest enemy we face. There are two types of pressure:

External: This is the pressure that comes from the opinions of others. I call it "people pressure." It often involves the pressure of time. For an example, someone will say, "You have to make a decision in three days." This type of demand can set the stage for extreme pressure. You feel pressured to make a decision now rather than later. There are some major decisions in life where we need to take time—days, weeks, or even months—to understand God's will and mind. There are other times when the Lord understands time restraints. He knows when you truly do need to make a decision and will make His will known in accordance with the need you have. Therefore, never allow yourself to be pressured by others if you know that God is prompting you to wait. On the other hand, do not allow the enemy to hold you back from stepping forward to make a decision that is clearly God's best for you.

Internal: This comes when the Holy Spirit is coaching us to make a decision or to deal with a situation. Pressure in this way means we do not really have a clear guidance and direction for a decision that we are considering. It is God's way of saying, "Be patient. Don't yield to the pressure of those externally who would force you to make a decision when you are not ready." You may not have all the facts. Therefore, when the pressure increases, tell the Lord, "I'm Your servant. It is my duty [you are duty-bound to be obedient to God] to obey You. In order for me to do this, I need to know Your will for my situation. I cannot follow unless You are guiding me. Please open my heart and mind to Your plan and show me exactly what You want me to do. So, Lord, I'm waiting patiently for You, refusing to be pressured into anything. I have cleared my mind and my heart of any known sin or personal desire. Now, Lord, tell me what You want me to do" (Stanley, Charles F., *How to Let God Solve Your Problems?* 2008, by Great Commission Media, pp. 114–115).

In the book *How to Listen to God*, Charles Stanley speaks on the topic "Is God still talking?" He states the following:

> How God Speaks Today
>
> We can be thankful that God is still in the communication business. He employs four principal methods of revealing Himself to the contemporary believer.
>
> Through His Word
>
> The Lord's primary way of speaking to us today is through His Word. We already have the complete revelation of God. He doesn't need to add anything else to this Book. The revelation of God is the unfolding truth of God by God about Himself. It is the inspiration of the Holy Spirit controlling the minds of men who penned the pages that make up the Bible. The Bible is the breath of God breathed upon those men that they might know the truth.
>
> Yes, the most assured way we can know we hear from God is through His Word. When we face difficulties and heartaches, rather than seek the counsel of a friend, we should first go to the Scriptures.
>
> Through the Holy Spirit
>
> A second method God uses to speak to us today is through the Holy Spirit. In fact, the primary way Jesus spoke in the New Testament was through the Holy Spirit. Today, God still speaks to our spirits through His Spirit who now lives, dwells, and abides in us.

HOW PRAYER CAN WALK YOU THROUGH THE STORMS IN YOUR LIFE

If we walk in the Spirit daily, surrendered to His power, we have the right to expect anything we need to hear from God. The Holy Spirit living within us and speaking to us ought to be the natural, normal lifestyle of believers. We can claim His presence, direction, and guidance.

Through other people

A third way God speaks to us is through other people. This became clear to me during a prolonged illness.

One Sunday, I became very ill and had to go to the hospital. All I could do was sleep the first two days. On the third day, my wife came to visit, and we began talking because God had impressed upon my heart the need to go back to the very beginning of my life and review it up to the present point. I felt He had something to show me, and I needed my wife to help me see it.

Every afternoon, we talked. We talked the rest of that week, and all of the next week, and all of the next week. For three weeks, she wrote and she listened. Toward the end of the third week, my wife looked over a mountain of paper where she had recorded the conversations and said, "I believe God has shown me what the problem is." When she told me, the problem in my life became clear to me for the first time. God absolutely spoke through my wife and showed me something that brought about one of the most dramatic changes in my ministry. Had I not listened, I would have missed a magnificent blessing.

That is why we need to be very careful about what we say. Recognizing that we can be used as God's spokespersons should cause us to soberly examine our dialogue. Perhaps God has a message for the listener that He has chosen us to deliver, and our talking about the weather or a football game would detract from that message. Thus, we should seek to be alert, sensitive, and available to God's voice.

Through circumstances

A fourth way God speaks to us is through circumstances. I believe those weeks in the hospital were engineered by God so that I could hear what He was saying. Such circumstances take on many forms. Sometimes, it is a failure. Sometimes, it is a success. Sometimes, it is a disappointment. Sometimes, it is a tragedy, but God uses all circumstances in life to speak to us (Stanley, Charles. *How to Listen to God*. Thomas Nelson, 2002, pp. 13–17).

16

What to Do When the Storm Is Over?

When the storm is over, you keep praising God and telling Him how awesome He is. Thank Him for your journey and all the people who prayed for you during this difficult time. You can look back over your past and see your progress in your journal, so keep writing.

Rest in the presence of God and ask Him to show you how to apply what you have learned to your life and share your testimony. Try to learn everything you can from the storm so you will be prepared for the next one. Once again, raise your hands, praise God, rest, and stay in the Word, which is your spiritual food.

Remember, practice makes perfect, so keep a positive attitude and allow the Holy Spirit to guide you as you walk through the next storm with prayer. Always remember God has His perfect time to answer you.

Turning Your Lemon into Lemonade

God always tells us that He is here to help us. He has allowed us to go through this storm. Now, it is your testimony time. I want to encourage you to tell your story so that you can encourage someone else. This is just another way God makes our lemon into lemonade.

By telling others your testimony, it can save headaches and pain for others. It will help other people see how you walked through the journey when they are faced with a similar situation, and they will think twice before they react. Even in difficult situations that people do not make the right decisions, and they hear your testimony, it will encourage them not to choose the wrong route because they will not want to experience the pain you shared with them.

The pain that you have gone through has surely made you stronger and your faith has increased in God. Your pain is turned into a blessing. Keep watching to see what God is up to next in your life; it will be good.

It Is Time to Turn the Pain into Ministry

The storm is over, and it is time to practice what you have learned. This is a great opportunity to turn your pain into ministry. There are so many people who need a support group or whatever kind of ministry you want to provide. When we go through painful times in our lives, we can give birth to a ministry that other people can benefit from.

I enjoy volunteering in the prison, and it is awesome to see how talented these people are. When they get out and are placed back into society, they become part of the local prison ministry outreach program, so they will have the support they need. The ones that are faithful will ask if they can go into the prisons to teach the other inmates. I listen to them play the instruments and sing from their hearts; it puts a smile on my face.

Since I enjoy praying, it feels like something natural for me to do. When people would call me and ask me to pray for them, I would be thrilled and say, "Of course, I will pray for you." As I continue to grow and understand the importance of prayer, I am glad I can use it to benefit other people. Life is about helping someone else, not focusing on my own needs. Since I like prayer, here are a few things that I do to help other people:

1. I have prayer meetings in my home.

2. I provide a phone line where people can request prayer twenty-four seven.
3. I like to coordinate small groups on prayer.
4. I like to invite people to go with me to other prayer meetings in the city.

A small group setting is a good place to teach a class on prayer; people can be open with questions they want to ask. You can have a book that the class can use as a guide. This is also a great setting to teach people how to pray and discuss the types of prayer. You can see if the group would like to have prayer partners. I enjoyed having a prayer partner; we had a set time to call each other to pray together once a week. Then, we exchanged prayer requests, and we prayed for that list until we called each other at the next appointed time. We held each other accountable, and we stuck to our commitment.

Some people enjoy the feeling of closeness from a small group setting so that they continue to seek other's groups. Once you are trained, you may want to teach a class on how to start a small group in your church or home. We never know how God will use us for His work.

We all experience pain in different ways, so we can use whatever type of ministry we want to use to help others. Here are a few ways that people can benefit from ministry. Whatever your misery is, turn it into a benefit for other people.

1. An inmate was released from prison; he has turned his life around and is a pastor. He is going into the prison to teach others about Christ.
2. You want to provide meals for people who are returning home from a hospital stay because you saw a need for this when you were in the hospital.
3. You recently became homeless, living in the shelter, and now, you are back on your feet. You want to provide meals and clothing for the homeless.
4. You had a problem with alcohol or drugs; you have been sober for years. Now, you are volunteering your time at an

AA group meeting. You go into the school system to help educate children not to use alcohol and drugs.
5. You were abused as a child; now, you are teaching classes on abuse prevention.
6. If you are unable to find someone to keep your child so you can work, open up a small day-care center in your home.
7. If you had to deal with some severe suffering in your life, you can teach others how to walk through the pain of suffering.
8. I once read about a boy growing up with barely anything to eat after his father left them. He decided to start a food pantry later in life. What a blessing.

17

Why Am I Glad God Chastises Me?

As a representative of God, I am still in training. He is only showing His love for me. My life would be a mess if He did not allow me to experience pain and have all kinds of difficulties. I would not know how to treat people or love them the way God wants me to. I would not have any idea of what it means to wait for certain things and be able to appreciate them.

When God disciplines me, it teaches me more about Him. I get to know Him on a deeper level. My faith increases to a new level. His discipline teaches me how to have a deeper dependency on Him. His love continues to leave me in awe.

God gets to take this body of mine and chip off piece by piece however He wants to, in order to polish me. He not only makes me better; He makes me more beautiful on the inside. When He shapes me and molds me, I am able to be used for His kingdom, and the good that He places inside of me can be shared with others. He brings the best out of me. This is called the blessings—the benefits of God's love, mercy, and grace.

Although I can see some progress in developing patience, I have a long way to go. Patience is a hard thing, but it is something we all must learn. We live in a world where everything is so fast paced, and we want things instantly. God does not work that way. He wants me to have the patience to glorify Him in all things. I catch myself from time to time at red lights, waiting for them to turn green. I have begun to start counting to twenty-five, and then another twenty-five, until the light turns green, so I will not lose my patience. This shows you that God is still pruning me piece by piece, and of course, it is what I need.

When I am in a storm now, I tell myself God is up to something. This keeps my focus on Him; it allows me to smile and see the joy in the midst of the storm. I can always find something to be thankful for during the storm. I look for ways to use my resources from God during the storms and live more at peace so I can have a good night's sleep. I need a good night's sleep because some of my storms are very draining. They can take a lot of time and energy, and I need to be refreshed in my walk. I want to live for God, be strong, and show others that I can walk through the battles with His tools and use them toward my advantage.

18

Keep the Dream Alive

Keeping the dream alive is depending on God to help us get to our destiny. It is about learning why God placed us on Earth and what we are to do while living here. These are questions we need to be in prayer with God about, and spending time in the Word to learn more about Him. I want us all to have a dream from God because He wants us to reach our full potential for Him. God provides everything we need to keep this dream alive. We must have faith in Him to walk out our dream.

If God has given you a dream, please do not let it slip away. Ask Him to show you what it is He wants to do through you. Let Him know you are willing to be trained. Yes, this means going through in order to get to the place where God wants you to be. God may just be waiting for you, so spend time talking with Him about this.

God has given me a dream of having an outreach center. This will be a center where people from all walks of life can participate. I believe in doing ministry where I am, until God places me where He wants me to be. This is why I like having my house open to small group meetings or prayer meetings; this is what outreach is all about. It is like I have a mini outreach ministry in my home. I look at it this way: if I desire to have an outreach ministry full time, what am I doing to show God I want to reach my dream? I am actually working where I am until I get to the dream I desire. God sees my heart, and as long as I am in His will, He will provide everything I need to get there. I have the faith I need to trust Him; He did not bring me this far to leave me.

We all know the saying, "Where He guides, He always provides." This is very true; we just have to step out in faith and trust Him. After all the pain and headaches I have gone through in my journey, my trust is totally in God. He wants us to get to a point in our lives where we have total dependence on Him. If I do my part, He will do the rest. I need to stay focused on my dream and keep moving forward.

Anyone who knows me understands that I love coffee, so yes, coffee will be available as part of this outreach ministry. I think coffee is something we can enjoy as we pray and reminisce about what God is doing in our lives. When we share with others, it just seems to bring something alive in us. We leave each other feeling motivated with a stronger desire to live for Christ. Here is a list of some things I would like to provide for the community when God is ready:

1. A place where people can come for prayer
2. A place where children can have tutoring classes after school
3. Spiritual classes for the adults and children
4. A spiritual library where people can come in and read different books and materials about walking with Christ
5. A counseling program
6. Classes offered on financial management
7. Support groups for adults

When I reach my destiny, it will be a great day in the Lord because I know this is something dear to my heart, and God knows me better than I know myself. He has designed me for a special assignment, and I want to reach it to the fullest. I know God created me and gave me talents and gifts that are only for me. I am standing on His promises and waiting for Him to speak to me about the next step in my life. I look forward to Him sharing with me what He has in store because I know God has something good in mind. I want to live for Him, and when my life is over on this side, I want heaven to be my home. I want to hear the words of Matthew 25:21–23), "Well done, good and faithful servant! You have been faithful with a few things; I will put you in charge of many things. Come and share your Master's happiness!"

19

Conclusion

I understand that prayer is powerful, passionate, and needs to be persistent in my life. I need to persevere throughout the trial, stand on God's promises, and wait until He answers. I must faithfully PUSH—pray until something happens—because I know God is up to something good in my life. I do not want to miss the blessing, so I will hold on and never give up.

We all know storms are inevitable; we have no control over what will occur in our lives. We have the assurance that God will give us His peace as we walk and trust Him through the process. We must seek direction from God and follow His will for the perfect peace that only He can give. We need to feed ourselves spiritually, pray daily, and give God thanks for the opportunity we have to grow closer to Him. We must keep a positive attitude in the storm, because storms can either make us or break us, depending on how we respond. It is very important to ask God what it is that He wants us to learn from the storm.

We must take advantage of the benefits designed to assist us in the storms we face. God is waiting for us; He is looking for us to call on Him so He can assist us. When we tap into the benefits from God, we can have confidence in our walk, and we can sleep at night and have the peace that passes all understanding. God is an amazing God. He opens doors that we thought had been closed; He gives us energy when we feel that we cannot go on. He takes away our worries and anxieties and replaces them with joy, smiles, and blessings.

What a great blessing this is! Lord, help us to take full advantage of these resources.

God allows us to experience all kinds of pain, disappointments, and financial problems so we can spend time getting to know Him better. He wants us to have a personal relationship with Him and to truly understand who He is and what He can do for us. He speaks to us in different ways, and He knows what it takes to get our attention. He will use whatever method He needs for us to yield to His will. We can save ourselves a lot of headaches, if we only follow His will and not try to do things in our own power. When we try to take things in our own hands, we are asking for more trouble. We should be willing to follow the Lord's plan without having to go through all the unnecessary pain.

We know every day is not going to be sunshine, and storms will keep on coming. We need to learn how to live in the storm and survive it in a healthy way. We need to look at storms as a learning tool—a way to search for understanding and to gain patience in the midst of the storm. If we stay calm in the storm, approach it with wisdom, and allow the Holy Spirit to guide us; we will succeed with joy. We can thank God for the journey, get some rest, and be ready to learn from the next storm that will surely come.

God wants to assist us in managing our storms so they will not manage us. Life is much better with the Master in charge, so we do not have to carry this load alone. Once we understand how to use God's benefits, we can obtain the faith we need to walk with confidence through the storms. This will help us to press on and be thankful as we walk this journey. We have a Father that will go all the way with us, keeping us strong and depending on Him. He is a God of many chances; we just need to take Him at His Word.

If you feel that you need some encouragement as you are walking through the storm, feel free to ask God for what you need. Remember, He is waiting for you to seek Him. Take the time to share your feelings and ask Him for encouragement. Watch how He responds to you and be ready to receive what He sends your way.

Sometimes, when we ask for encouragement, it may be a phone call, a visit from someone, or simply driving down the street and a song comes on your radio that reminds you of what you have been praying about. We know God is always working on our behalf. He works behind the scenes. When He is ready to reveal things to us, we need to be ready and accept them with thanksgiving and praise. God did not provide this walk for us to be alone. He will carry us through the journey if we allow Him.

We must remember, prayer is something that needs to be a natural thing in our lives.

It is our relationship with God. His Word brings us purpose in life. The Word brings comfort and hope to God's children, and we need to take advantage of it. The Word causes spiritual growth, and this is what helps us to be able to walk through these storms. It gives us the faith to hold on when God is working the night shift, and we are not able to see what He is doing in our lives.

My prayers will be with each and every one who reads this book. I want to encourage you to keep praying, no matter what life brings your way. God is able to handle your pain and disappointments. He is in the waiting room, just a prayer away. Let go of your life and allow Him to have His way with you. He is the taxi driver, and we are in the back seat, following the directions of the Holy Spirit, so we can succeed on this journey and reach our destiny.

References

Carothers, Merlin. 1997. *From Fear to Faith*. Foundation of Praise.

CBN.com. 2019. *Keys to Powerful Living: Peace*. The Christian Broadcasting Network, Inc.

Couchman, Judith. 1992. *Lord, Have You Forgotten Me?* Word Publishing.

DeLashmutt, Gary. *Asking According to God's Will*. https://www.xenos.org/teaching/?teaching=1032.

Dixon, Francis. *The Promise of Peace in the Midst of the Storm*. https://www.wordssoflife.co.uk/bible-studies-/qstudy-8-the-promise-of-peace-in-the-midst-of-storm.

Dollar, Creflo. *The Battle Isn't Ours to Fight*. https://creflodollarministries.org.

Evans, Tony. *When God Allows Your Trial*. https://tonyevans.org/.

Fairchild, Mary. *What Does the Bible Say About Prayer?* https://www.thoughtco.com.

Franklin, Jentezen. 2017. *Right People, Right Place, Right Plan Devotional: Discerning the Voice of God*. Whitaker House.

Hayford, Jack. *Bring Your Struggling to the Cross*. httns://www.jackhayford.org/teaching/articles/bring-your-struggling-to-the-cross.

Hopler, Whitney. *God Walks with You Through the Valleys*. https://www.crosswalk.com/faith/spiritual-life/God-walks-with-you-through-the-valleys-13.

James, Rick. *The Significance of Trials*. https://www.cru.org/us/en/blog/life-and-relationships/hardships/the-significance-of-trials.h.

Jones, David R. *The Benefits of Trials*. http://www.bible-facts.info/commentaries/nt/james/james1v3 12.htm.

Jones, Jenn. *Keeping Faith in Hard Times*. http://goingbyfaith.com/keeping-faith-in-trials-temptation-and-tough-times.

Krejcir, Richard J. Dr. *God Really Does Have a Purpose Behind Your Problems!* http://www.discipleshiptools.org/apps/articles/default.asp?articleid=37254, Merriam-Webster Online Dictionary.

Meyer, Joyce. 2017. *Be Anxious for Nothing*. Faith Words.

———. 2002. *Enjoying Where You Are on the Way to Where You Are Going*. Warner Books.

———. 2003. *Knowing God Intimately*. Faith Words.

———. *Learning to Live by Faith*.

Mustard Seed Faith. www.adevotion.org/archive/mustard-seed-faith/2016/1018.

Omartian, Stormie and Hayford, Jack. 2003. *The Power of Praying Together*.

Osteen, Joel. 2009. *It's Your Time*. New York: Free Press.

———. 2015. *Your Best Life Now: 7 Steps to Living at Your FULL Potential*. Faith Words.

———. 2019. *A Seed of Hope*. https://www.joelosteen.com.

Rogers, Adrian. *Love Worth Finding: Finding Peace in the Midst of Your Storm*. http://www.lwf.org.

Rush, Terry. 1995. *God Will Make a Way*. Howard Publishing Company.

Stanley, Charles. 2002. *How to Listen to God?* Thomas Nelson.

———. 2004. *Walking Wisely*. Thorndike Press.

———. 2008. *How to Let God Solve Your Problems?* Great Commission Media.

———. 2005. *Living Close to God*. Thomas Nelson.

———. 2008. *How to Handle Adversity?* Thomas Nelson.

———. *Weathering the Storms*. https://www.intouch.org.

———. Wisdom in the Midst of Trials, https://www.intouch.org.

Thompson, Andrew C. *ACTS: 4 Kinds of Prayer for the Christian*. https://www.seedbed.com/acts-4-kinds-of-prayer-for-the-christian.

Velarde, Robert. *Prayer Has Its Reasons*. https://www.focusonthefamily.com.

Vinson, Christina. 2015. *God's Peace for When You Can't Sleep*. Thomas Nelson.

Webster's Online Dictionary 1828.

Woods, B. W. 1982. *Christians in Pain*. Baker Book House.

She's a living testimony that God's wisdom, strength, and abilities reside in us, but they don't come out in a place of convenience. They don't come out in a place of comfort; they don't come out when everything is easy. It is through the squeezes of life that our potentials come out; it is through the afflictions of our circumstances that the depth of God's wisdom is released for us. For this reason, Ms. Farley did not faint nor did she abandon her project. Ms. Essie Farley, thanks for being faithful in prayer, and that's why you have successfully ridden the storms of adversity and arrived at your desired destination.

—Dr. Kenneth R. Greene

A strong proponent of living in the footprints of Jesus as she lifts others up. She is an excellent example of strength and encouragement in her Christian walk. She is a strong Christian woman of God.

—Glenda Watson

For as long as I have known Ms. Essie Farley, she has demonstrated herself to be a James 1 servant. Her passion for prayer and holiness have been her pursuit. She is always quick to hear, slow to speak, and slow to anger because of her personal relationship with Jesus Christ. Ms. Farley is a straightforward woman of God whom I highly respect and honor and am grateful to God for her authentic friendship.

—Rose Marie Moreno

About the Author

Essie Farley was born and raised in Putnam County, Eatonton Georgia.

Essie Farley is the founder and president of Essence House of Prayer, which is a volunteer prayer-line ministry, which was established on August 24, 2011. She was the prayer minister of the Metro Church of Christ in Dallas, Texas before moving to Corpus Christi, Texas. She attends Kings Crossing Church of Christ in Corpus Christi, Texas, where she is active with the lady's ministry and prison ministry. She is a volunteer chaplain for Bay Area Hospital.

Essie Farley has taken her pain, disappointments, failures, and everything else to the Father in prayer. She prays, listens, and waits for God to speak to her through the Holy Spirit. Essie Farley shares that we should view our problems as opportunities. God uses these opportunities to bless other people. She knows God has placed her on this Earth to do something. This is why she has been praying, "Lord, what have you created me to be?" She always asks God to reveal the answer to her prayers in a crystal-clear way, so she can understand on her level.

Essie Farley has been a social worker for thirty years. She also worked as a nursing home administrator. She is a graduate of Southwestern Christian College and Lubbock Christian University. She resides in the beautiful city of Corpus Christi, Texas.

CPSIA information can be obtained
at www.ICGtesting.com
Printed in the USA
LVHW111356240721
693586LV00003B/69